FAMOUS CRICKETERS OF MIDDLESEX

FAMOUS CRICKETERS OF MIDDLESEX

DEAN HAYES

Foreword by
Denis Compton

SPELLMOUNT
Tunbridge Wells

Titles in the Spellmount/Nutshell Cricket list:

The Test Match Career of Geoffrey Boycott
by C D Clark
The Test Match Career of Sir Jack Hobbs
By Clive Porter
Cricket Anthology
by Samuel J Looker
The Test Match Career of Walter Hammond
by Derek Lodge
Kent Cricketing Greats
by Dean Hayes
The Test Match Career of Ted Dexter
by Dean Hayes
The Lord's Test
by Steven Lynch
Famous Cricketers of Essex
by Dean Hayes

First Published in the UK in 1992 by
Spellmount Ltd
12 Dene Way, Speldhurst
Tunbridge Wells, Kent TN3 ONX

British Library Cataloguing in Publication Data
Hayes, Dean 1949 –
Famous Cricketers of Middlesex – (Famous county cricketers).
1. Middlesex (England). Cricket
I. Title II. Series
796.3580922

ISBN 0–946771–19–7

Design by David Morley-Clarke
Typeset by DMC Associates, London

Printed in Great Britain by Biddles Ltd, Guildford, Surrey

CONTENTS

ACKNOWLEDGEMENTS 6
SELECT BIBLIOGRAPHY 7
FOREWORD 8
INTRODUCTION 9
GUBBY ALLEN 21
GRAHAM BARLOW 24
DON BENNETT 26
BERNARD BOSANQUET 27
MIKE BREARLEY 30
SYD BROWN 33
GEORGE BURTON 35
ROLAND BUTCHER 36
DENIS COMPTON 38
NORMAN COWANS 42
WAYNE DANIEL 44
PAUL DOWNTON 46
JACK DURSTON 48
PHIL EDMONDS 50
BILL EDRICH 52
JOHN EMBUREY 57
BOB GALE 59
MIKE GATTING 60
NIGEL HAIG 63
J T HEARNE 65
JOHN W HEARNE 68
PATSY HENDREN 70
RON HOOKER 74
HARRY LEE 75
GREGOR MacGREGOR 77
GEORGE MANN 79
FRANK MANN 81
ALAN MOSS 83
JOHN MURRAY 85
TIMOTHY O'BRIEN 87
PETER PARFITT 89
IAN PEEBLES 91
JOHN PRICE 93
FRED PRICE 95
CLIVE RADLEY 97
JOHN RAWLIN 99
JACK ROBERTSON 100
WALTER ROBINS 103
ERIC RUSSELL 105
MIKE SELVEY 107
JIM SIMS 109
WILF SLACK 111
JIM SMITH 113
MIKE SMITH 115
GREVILLE STEVENS 117
ANDREW STODDART 118
FRANK TARRANT 121
FRED TITMUS 124
ALBERT TROTT 126
ISAAC WALKER 129
VYELL WALKER 130
PELHAM WARNER 132
JOHN WARR 135
JACK YOUNG 137
APPENDICES 139
STATISTICAL ANALYSIS 139
TOP TENS 140
BATTING AVERAGES 142
BOWLING AVERAGES 143
WICKET KEEPING 144

ACKNOWLEDGEMENTS

I am greatly indebted to the following for their help in the compilation of this book:

Joe Hardstaff MBE (Middlesex Secretary) and Denis Compton who has kindly written the foreword. Further thanks to Peter Stafford (ex-Bolton League Secretary) for his continued support.

The illustrations were kindly provided by Middlesex CCC and the Curator at Lord's.

The author also wishes to thank Mr Derek Lodge for his help in compiling the statistics.

SELECT BIBLIOGRAPHY

Mike Brearley: *The Art of Captaincy* (Hodder and Stoughton) 1985
Norman G Brett-Jones: *Middlesex* (Robert Hale) 1951
H W Lee and L Thompson: *Forty Years of English Cricket* (Clerke and Cochran) 1948
Terence Prittie: *Middlesex – The County Series* (Convoy) 1951
David Frith: *My Dear Victorious Stod* (Lutterworth Press) 1977
David Lemon; *the History of Middlesex CCC* (Middlesex CCC) 1948
Nigel Haig: *Middlesex CCC 1921–1947* (Middlesex CCC) 1948
plus various Cricketer Magazines; Wisden Cricket Monthlies: Wisdens: and Middlesex Yearbooks.

FOREWORD

Middlesex players enjoy a unique advantage in the cricketing world: Lord's, the headquarters of cricket and most famous of cricket grounds, is our home ground. Lord's is the place to play, to make runs and take wickets; Lord's is where it really matters in a cricketing sense. Thus, many visitors (certainly those playing at Lord's for the first time) tend to be overawed by the sense of occasion as they tread the hallowed turf. It follows that Middlesex, the home team, has an enormous advantage.

At the same time, most matches at Lord's are played in the glare of intense publicity; notable performances are reported fully by the media and the more successful Middlesex players tend to become better known than those who play in the provinces. Thus, perhaps one should not be surprised that so many Middlesex players become famous.

Having been associated with Middlesex for more than 55 years, I am privileged to have played with many of the players described in this book and I have known and admired most of the rest. All in their various ways have been, and some still are, famous Middlesex cricketers. Reading the pen portraits in this book, many memories came flooding back, of people, of places, of incidents during my cricketing life. Every one gave a great deal to the game, to Middlesex and in many cases to England; they all shared a sense of pride in being Middlesex players and they have all loved the game of cricket. Fame has been thrust upon them.

Denis Compton.

Denis Compton CBE

INTRODUCTION

The history of Middlesex County Cricket Club as we know it today really dates from 2 February 1864, when a county club was founded at a meeting attended by seventy-five people at the *London Tavern* at Bishopsgate. On the previous November 1863 a group of men, headed by John and V E Walker, C Gordon, C Hillyard and W Nicholson had surveyed a ground in the Islington Cattle Market Enclosure and this became the first home of Middlesex County Cricket. The first county secretary was Mr Hillyard; Mr Nicholson became Honorary Treasurer and the Walker brothers were appointed joint-captains.

From 1864 to 1873 there was no County Championship, although some team was generally accepted as the best of the year.

In 1866 Middlesex won six and drew one of the eight matches they played and were nominally the best county, but their finances were in a poor state and they had frequent disagreements with the Islington landlord. One example; he was apt to use the ground for races on Whit Monday! Middlesex gave up the tenancy after the 1868 season.

During that 1866 season they had a double win over Lancashire and twice beat Surrey by an innings. The main men of this the county's first success, were roughly the same as for the first five years of their existence; V E Walker headed the batting averages with 52, whilst R D Walker and J T Hearne were also leading lights. The other distinguished members of that 1866 side were wicket-keeper R Bisset-Halliwell, G Howitt (a bowler who played for Nottinghamshire also that season) and J J Sewell, a forcing batsman.

V E Walker played for England against Surrey in 1859, taking all ten Surrey wickets for 74 and scoring 108 not out in England's second innings. He also took 10 for 65 playing for Middlesex against Lancashire and was thought of as the greatest lob-bowler in the history of the game. He was one of four Walker brothers from Southgate who played in Middlesex's first match after their foundation in 1864. In 1868 Isaac Walker played a great innings of 165 for the Gentlemen against the Players, hitting two sixes, three fives and 17 fours.

The county played two matches in 1869, both against Surrey. One of these matches was at Lord's; in fact two matches against Surrey were all that Middlesex could manage the following two seasons also.

In 1870, Middlesex found a new home at Lillie Bridge, West Brompton, on the Amateur Athletic Club running ground. the move didn't meet with much success, as the turf was rarely in a fit condition for playing and a dry summer only made matters worse. The first match at Lillie Bridge took place the following season and was the only home game of the season! This was despite the undoubted talent of the county's many gifted amateurs. There was a suggestion at a General Meeting held on January

1871, that there wasn't really room for a Middlesex XI in London, as well as Surrey and the MCC However, only thirteen members turned up and so the defeatist motion was lost by a single vote. At the meeting, P M Thornton became Honorary Secretary, a position he was to hold until 1899.

By 1871 however, there was an increase in membership and Middlesex realised that a more central ground would certainly encourage attendances to rise and the club's finances to recover. Until the County could afford to pay for more professionals, it would have to depend to a great extent on its amateurs

In those years leading up to the first year in which there was a recognised County Championship, there were some notable performances, the best being W H Hadow's innings of 217 in 1871, playing against the MCC of which W G Grace was a member and Alfred Shaw on the ground staff; Middlesex won the match by an innings.

At a General Meeting of the Club on 9 February 1872, it was decided to transfer their headquarters to the Prince's Ground at Hans Place, Kensington. The move brought financial stability to Middlesex. They stayed at Prince's until the end of the 1876 season. Meanwhile, they had turned down a proposal that they should move to Alexandra Park and another offer from the MCC in 1875.

The summer of 1873 is generally considered as the first year in which there was a recognised County Championship, I D Walker being the best batsman with 92 runs at an average of 43.50.

At the end of the 1876 season, Middlesex had a disagreement with the Proprietor's of Prince's over financial matters and so they held an Extraordinary General Meeting on 7 November 1876. At this meeting, it was accepted that Middlesex should play four matches at Lord's and should take all gate-money and defray all expenses. The Middlesex members were to have access to the pavilion when the county was playing a match. In fact, P M Thornton, the honorary secretary stated he would not carry on unless the club went to Lord's.

Initially, Middlesex paid nothing for the privilege of playing at Lord's, but by 1885 they had begun to make a financial contribution to the MCC; a more definite financial arrangement was agreed between the two clubs four years later.

In the 1870s and 1880s at different times, Middlesex possessed a great array of talented stroke-makers. They must have been a good side to watch with ID and V E Walker, A J Webbe, the Lyttletons, the Studds, Sir Timothy O'Brien, F G J Ford and A E Stoddart.

In 1883, I D Walker and Alfred Lyttleton put on 324 for the second wicket against Gloucestershire at Clifton, 226 of the runs coming in an hour and three-quarters after lunch.

In 1884, Timothy O'Brien hit 119 against Gloucestershire and produced two dashing innings against Surrey, though it was four years later that he really came to the fore. After playing against Yorkshire at the beginning of that 1888 season, he dropped out until mid-July, returning to score 482 runs in 11 innings at an average of 53.55. This was a remarkable feat, when one remembers how much lower the scale of scoring was in those days.

In 1886, A E Stoddart hit 485 in a little over six hours playing for Hampstead against Stoics, following it three days later with 207 against Blackheath.

In 1887, A J Webbe who had succeeded I D Walker as captain two years earlier, scored 192 and 243 not out against Kent and Yorkshire respectively during the month of August.

Also, the appearance of George Burton, a slow bowler of great consistency, strengthened the side. In his ten full seasons for the county, he took 504 wickets at 16.83 runs each. In 1888, he took all ten Surrey wickets in the first innings at the Oval for 59. His figures may not look too impressive, but in the 1880s, the county had a short fixture programme.

J T Hearne was for more than two decades the mainstay of the Middlesex attack. He is one of only four bowlers in the history of the game to have taken over 3000 wickets.

The 1893 season brought some new records for Middlesex. J T Hearne took more wickets for the county than any previous bowler; Stoddart hit two centuries in the same match and reached 1000 runs in county matches alone and MacGregor behind the stumps, claimed 34 victims.

J T Hearne's best season was 1896, when he took 257 wickets. In fact, from 1891 – 1898, he took 924 wickets for Middlesex at a cost of 15·84 each. In 1899, he performed the hat-trick for England in the Leeds Test against Australia. He was ably supported by Yorkshire born J T Rawlin whose best season was 1894 when he took 104 wickets (90 for Middlesex). Others of note, were Jim Phillips, E A Nepean and C M Wells.

In 1894, counties such as Derbyshire, Essex, Leicestershire and Warwickshire and in 1895 Hampshire became first-class counties, so greatly expanding the county championship programme.

Middlesex had played plenty of good cricket in the years leading up to 1895 and had fully deserved to earn a place in the 'Big Six' of county cricket. Between the years 1896 and 1901 (with the exception of 1897) Middlesex had an excellent side and finished runners-up in the County Championship on three occasions. There were three reasons for the county's success:

First, Plum Warner had developed into one of the most consistent batsmen in England; secondly, Albert Trott, disgruntled at not being selected for the Australian side to tour England, migrated and qualified for Middlesex in 1898 and thirdly, as I mentioned earlier, the county possessed the batting strength of half-a-dozen amateurs, notably Andrew Stoddart and Timothy O'Brien.

After finishing runners-up in 1898, the county almost went one place better the following year, only a bad spell of three defeats and a draw stopped them from doing so. They were much more of a team in 1899 and Albert Trott became the first ever player to score over 1000 runs and take over 200 wickets in a season.

One match that season stands out, this was Middlesex's game with Somerset at Lord's. It was a remarkable match, Middlesex only scored 86, yet won by an innings inside a day! There was no play on the bank Holiday due to rain and when play did get under way on the second day, the wicket was treacherous. In fact, Somerset lost their first eight wickets for eight runs, but managed to reach 35. Middlesex gained a lead of 51 and then Trott proved unplayable as the West Country side were dismissed for 44, to give Middlesex victory by an innings and 7 runs.

The 1900 season saw A E Stoddart's farewell to the first-class game at Lords. Playing in J T Hearne's benefit match against Somerset, he hit his highest score in first-class cricket, 221 in his sides second innings. It was a season too, when B J T Bosanquet achieved what many considered his best performance with the bat scoring 136 and 139 against Leicestershire at Lord's.

After finishing as runners-up in 1901, the county won the championship two years later with a series of outstanding performances. The first three games were won by big margins and the run of county successes was punctuated only by draws caused by the bad weather.

In 1905, there was an important addition to the side in F A Tarrant, who like Trott came from Victoria to try his luck with Middlesex. In his first match, he scored 53 and had match figures of 10 for 47 against Somerset, later becoming the most consistent all-rounder in English cricket.

From 1907-1914, Tarrant never failed to make over 1000 runs and take over 100 wickets each season – this record of all-round consistency was only rivalled by Hirst and Rhodes.

Albert Trott, will always be remembered as the man who hit Monty Noble of Australia for a six that carried right over the pavilion at Lord's, but in 1907 he performed two hat-tricks in the same innings in his benefit match against Somerset

The 1907 season brought a happy change in Middlesex's form and from then until the outbreak of war in 1914, they were always a formidable side. The chief factor behind the revival in Middlesex's form was undoubtedly the captaincy of P F Warner. He had already led England with great success in 1903-04 in Australia and always got the best out of his men for he had a keen and penetrating mind, understanding fully the finer points of the game.

It was around this time that two young professionals by the names of Hendren and J W Hearne appeared on the scene; they did nothing sensational at first, but by 1910 they were both firmly established in the Middlesex line-up.

Perhaps the most interesting match of the 1908 season was that against the touring Philadelphian side, when the fixture was completed inside a single day. Tarrant and Trott bowled the tourists out in under an hour for 58. Middlesex fared slightly better, reaching 92 before Tarrant and Trott again bowled out the Philadelphian side for 55. The county side had little trouble in scoring the 22 runs needed for victory, but a certain Patsy Hendren, playing in only his fourth game for the county, scored 0 and 0.

In 1911 Middlesex probably had their best side ever, apart from their Championship years. J T Hearne at the age of 44 was again the best bowler in the side. J W Hearne and Tarrant both completed the cricketer's double. Warner, Hendren and F T Mann batted well, assisted by the two Littlejohns and W P Harrison, when they trounced Surrey in both matches that summer. At Lord's, Middlesex won by 350 runs and then by an innings at the Oval. Three years later, Middlesex and Surrey were neck and neck in the race for the Championship, but the county had to settle for second place, although they didn't lose a single match until the last week in July. The feature of this last season before the war, was the all-round cricket of Tarrant and J W Hearne. Between them, they scored almost 4000 runs and took 245 wickets. Against Essex at Leyton, Tarrant scored 250 not out, whilst J W Hearne hit an unbeaten 106 and had match figures of 14 for 146. At Old Trafford, Tarrant took 9 for 105 and 7 for 71 and then hit 101 out of the 145 runs Middlesex needed for victory.

In 1913 and 1914 and again in 1920, J W Hearne made over 2000 runs and took over 100 wickets. His all-round work achieving a great deal for the county when they won the Championship in 1920.

Patsy Hendren began the 1919 season by making a score of over 200 against the Champions of the year, Yorkshire, at Lord's and then following it a few weeks later with 201 against Hampshire. He ended the season with 1655 runs and finished second in the national batting averages. His greatest year was probably 1920, when he scored 2520 runs at an average of 61, and topped the national averages – a feat he also achieved in 1922 and 1923.

Middlesex won the County Championship in 1920, under the leadership of Pelham Warner. The club were in sixth place at the end of July, but then proceeded to win eight matches on the trot, including one by 4 runs against Yorkshire in a very exciting match at Bradford. When the county entertained Sussex at Lord's, it was the first time the first four batsmen in county cricket all scored a century. Middlesex totalled 543 for 4 (Warner 139; Lee 119; Hearne 116*; Haig 131). Strangely enough, the only time it has been equalled was again by Middlesex in 1923 against Hampshire at Southampton, when Lee, Dales, Hearne and Hendren all made centuries.

It all came down to the last match against Surrey at Lord's; Middlesex needing to win, as their main rivals Lancashire seemed certain to defeat Worcestershire (which they did).

At the end of the first day, Middlesex had scored 253 for 8, with Warner contributing a brave but slow 79. He was helped by Hendren (41) and Stevens (53) who had been at school only a year before. Surrey declared their innings at 341 for 9 with Sandham getting a superb 167 not out, leaving Middlesex an anxious forty-five minutes batting. On the Tuesday morning, Skeet and Lee continued to bat with confidence and by lunch at 1.30pm Middlesex were 199 for 0. they both fell soon afterwards to Hitch and when Warner declared at 3.40pm Surrey needed 244 to win in three hours. Fender obviously thought Surrey could win and with Hobbs and Sandham in outstanding form, who could blame him? Stevens and J W Hearne spun Middlesex to victory by 55 runs. Plum Warner was a national hero, such was the extent of county cricket's importance at that time and he was carried of Lord's, both physically and mentally on the wave of emotion.

The batting was led by Hendren and J W Hearne with Harry Lee, a good third string. JW also headed the bowling averages with 119 wickets at 16.80 supported by Durston (who had the best record of all his colleagues at Lord's), Haig and the Sinhalese, Dr. C H Gunasekera.

Middlesex won the title again in 1921, this time under the leadership of

Frank Mann, a most popular captain and renowned big-hitter. By an amazing coincidence, the title's outcome depended on the last match against Surrey at Lord's. Whereas they'd had to win in 1920, in 1921 they only needed to avoid defeat. Surrey batted first and scored 269, Durston taking 4 for 47. Middlesex collapsed and were dismissed for 132, just avoiding the follow-on. Haig's swing bowling gave Middlesex a fighting chance, taking 5 for 62, as Surrey were bowled out for 184. Middlesex needed 322 for victory and reached their target for the loss of four wickets both Twining and J W Hearne hitting centuries.

One of the most popular of Middlesex cricketers at the time was Patsy Hendren. His career had begun as early as 1907 and was to continue until 1937, when his beloved Middlesex finished in the runners-up spot for the third consecutive year.

In 1923, Hendren made over 3000 runs for the first time, scoring 13 hundreds. He was far ahead of the next batsman, Philip Mead of Hampshire in the national averages, averaging 77 to Mead's 59.

In 1924, Middlesex once again finished second this time to Yorkshire and perhaps would have won the title if Gloucestershire (Hammond, a magnificent 174 not out) hadn't provided an unexpected reverse.

The following year, Hendren played the leading part in the most memorable of matches when Middlesex visited Trent Bridge. Nottinghamshire batting first, scored 167; Middlesex faring worse and reaching 127. In their second innings, Nottinghamshire scored 461 and Middlesex were left with the impossible task of scoring 502 to win, in a little more than a day's play. Overnight, they had lost three of their batsmen for just 60 runs. Bruce with 103 and F T Mann with an unbeaten 101, both scored centuries, but it was Hendren who had hit three centuries in the previous three matches, who saw the side home in a little over six hours with a masterful innings of 206 not out.

Making his Middlesex debut in 1925, Walter Robins ranked as the most successful county captain since Plum Warner and probably tactically, the best that Middlesex have ever possessed. He was certainly one of the most attractive players in his generation. His first year as captain saw Middlesex finish third and then for the next three years, he kept them in second place, close to the leaders.

Though the team didn't meet with success in the late twenties, Hendren had two magnificent seasons, scoring 2784 runs (average 73) in 1927 and 331 runs (average 70) in 1928. In each season, he made 13 centuries and three times he scored over 200.

In 1929, Middlesex had another of those exceptional summers, this was due to an unforeseen bowling improvement. It was the first time that three amateur bowlers had taken over 100 wickets each during the season for Middlesex. Their figures were as follows:

	Runs	*Wkts*	*Ave*
I A R Peebles	2424	123	19.70
R W V Robins	3468	162	21.53
N E Haig	3118	129	24.17

Coupled to this, another amateur, G O Allen took all ten wickets for 40 runs in an innings against Lancashire at Lord's.

In the first half of the thirties, Middlesex struggled, missing players of the calibre of those who had played in the successful twenties. However, few people could have expected Middlesex to sink to almost bottom of the county table.

The few bright spots provided in those years were generally from Hendren. At the age of 44, he qualified for a third benefit match, a unique compliment in Middlesex history. In the county's five dark years, he made over 12,000 runs for an average of well over 50. During this difficult time, Middlesex tried hard to unearth new talent.

In 1934 however, came the first of the younger generation who wereto change the fortunes of Middlesex cricket. Jim Smith had been bowling in Minor County cricket for quite a few years, when at the age of 27, he made his Middlesex debut. In his very first season, he took 172 wickets for 18 runs each in what was a summer of high scores. He was one of the best fast bowlers the county have ever had; between 1934 and 1938, he took 699 wickets at 18.00 runs each, though he was to become renownedfor his fast scoring and prodigious hitting.

In 1935, there was even more of a revival in the county, when Walter Robins was appointed captain, having decided to come back to the game. The revival continued the following year, when Middlesex finished second to Derbyshire. The year of 1936 deserves to rank as Hendren's year. He was by now, 47 years of age and yet he made 525 more runs than anyone else in England. He made 2654 runs for an average of 47, with nine centuries.

In 1937, Middlesex would surely have won the Championship if they hadn't got off to a bad start. It was the beginning of the Edrich Compton partnership and the last season for Patsy Hendren. They came the closest to knocking Yorkshire from their perch at the top of the table, yet the county could only draw its last two games against Nottinghamshire and Surrey and so just missed out. Not to be outdone, Robins issued a challenge to Yorkshire for a game to be played on a neutral ground. The white-rose county duly accepted and beat Middlesex by an innings at the Oval. It may well have been a different story if such gifted Middlesex amateurs as Allen, Enthoven, Killick and Peebles had been able to play on a more regular basis.

Though the county finished second in the next two seasons, they missed Hendren, for even at 48 years of age, he had been the real sheet-anchor of the side.

In the last three seasons before the war, the contribution of Edrich and Compton can best be summed up by their respective performances.

		Edrich		*Compton*
1937	2154 runs	44.87 Av	1980 runs	47.14 Av
1938	2378 runs	52.84 Av	1868 runs	45.56 Av
1939	2186 runs	49.68 Av	2468 runs	56.09 Av
	6718 runs	49.04 Av	6316 runs	49.80 Av

When one considers that Edrich played in all of the 1938 Tests and Compton for four in 1938 and three in 1939, the county's performance in those two years was all the more remarkable. Much of Middlesex's success in the last few years before the war, was due to their inspirational captain and all-rounder, Robins. Both he and Jim Sims were outstanding wrist-spinners of this period. Yet perhaps the player to show most promise in this period was Jack Robertson who scored over 900 runs in 1938 and over 1000 in 1939 after being dismissed for 0 in his single innings in 1937.

The years leading up to the war, were happy ones in the county's history, coinciding with the revival in English cricket.

In the first four years after the war, Middlesex were far and away the best county side in the country.

In 1946, they finished second to an ageing Yorkshire side, owing their position to a tremendous finish to the season when seven of the last nine matches were won outright. They had the three fine batsmen that they'd had before the war in Compton, Edrich and Robertson, and Syd Brown who was a most efficient opener; the latter two improving out of all recognition the following summer. Perhaps the greatest improvement was that shown by J A Young, a slow left-hander who'd been tried several times before the war. He proved very hard to hit and less than two runs an over were scored off him. He bowled particularly well against the county champions, taking 8 for 33 when playing for the MCC at Scarborough and then having match figures of 12 for 72 at Lord's.

The disappointments of that season were wiped clean away by the triumphs of the following summer, when Middlesex won the Championship. Cricket history produced some unusual parallels. After the 1914-18 war, Yorkshire had won the first post-war title; Middlesex took over the mantle the season after and each summer the respective Middlesex captain was playing his last full season of first-class cricket.

The county's achievement was all the more remarkable, for they had several of their best players absent through representative calls. Even so, of the nine matches played when they were under strength, they won seven. Yet it was when they were at full strength that they showed unbeatable form. Four matches were won by an innings and with their three top batsmen in the side, they scored at a phenomenal rate. When they played Surrey at the Oval, they ended the day on 537 for 2. The big three – Robertson, Edrich and Compton all scored centuries and Syd Brown only failed by two runs. If he had reached his hundred, the county would have repeated their unique record of twice having all their first four men over the century mark.

With Walter Robins at the helm, they took the country by storm. It was one of the hottest summers of this century and a most magnificent one for the Middlesex 'twins'. In all matches, Denis Compton scored 3816 runs with 18 centuries and topped the national averages with 90.85. Bill Edrich scored 3539 runs with 12 centuries at an average of 80.43. They were well supported by Jack Robertson, who hit 2760 runs and Syd Brown with 2078 runs. These brilliant batsmen made their runs quickly enough for a modest bowling attack to get the opposition out. The bowling attack consisted mainly of Laurie Gray, a fast-medium bowler and two spinners, Jack Young and Jim Sims. Both Compton and Edrich chipped in with useful contributions.

As a finale to the county's most successful season in their history, Middlesex met and defeated the Rest of England at the Oval in September. It was only the third occasion that the Champion County had succeeded in beating the full strength Rest of England.

Middlesex after losing Brown and Robertson to Bedser cheaply, totalled 543 with Compton scoring a magnificent 246 and Edrich 180, both stumped by Godfrey Evans off the bowling of Gloucestershire's Tom Goddard. The Rest of England were dismissed for 246 and then for 317 after following-on, leaving Middlesex just 21 to get.

As Plum Warner had done in 1921, Walter Robins handed the captaincy on to George Mann, the son of Frank Mann who followed Warner.

In fact, George Mann may well (like his father) have led Middlesex to the title in his first season, but he had to settle for third place. It would have been different if Edrich, Compton and Young hadn't been playing for England during vital county games. It was in this 1948 season, that Compton (252 not out) and Edrich (168 not out) put on 424 in four hours against Somerset at Lord's, establishing a new England record.

In 1949, with the county still under the charge of Mann they were back on top, finishing the season as joint-winners with Yorkshire. This was due in the main to the usually strong batting, with Jack Robertson setting up a new Middlesex record with an innings of 331 not out against Worcestershire. In the last game of that season, Compton hit a brave and brilliant undefeated 97 against Derbyshire, when their bowlers in the shape of Copson, Gladwin and Jackson seemed certain to come out on top. The 1949 season saw Fred Titmus at the age of 16, playing his first match – it was a career that was to span five decades and 64 matches.

The next few years proved to be a difficult period in the county's history. Inevitably, some of the giants from the pre-war days began to lose a little of their glitter. Denis Compton's playing days were shortened by the knee trouble which had required an operation in 1950 and Jim Sims played his last game at the age of 48 in 1952, He had taken 1579 wickets and scored 8983 runs. There were no title successes, but the counties general record was consistently good. They had been keeping high in the table, largely because they finished such a high proportion of their matches. In 1952, John Murray replaced Leslie Compton behind the stumps, dismissing 122 batsmen in a career that extended to 1975.

No truly great players came along to replace Compton and Edrich, though a successor to Robertson was found in the form of Eric Russell, a polished opening batsman. Another batsman to join Middlesex from Norfolk was Peter Parfitt, a top-class left-hander and a superb slip-fielder. Middlesex though possessed arguably the best fast-bowling attack in the country, with Alan Moss, John Warr and John Price, who would have done even better if he'd managed to avoid some of his injuries. There were others pressing their claims; Don Bennett, Ron Hooker, at that time primarily a batsman, but later developing into a medium-pace bowler of great value to the county and Bob Gale, a tall left-handed batsman who often took opposing attacks apart and was unlucky not to play for England.

The most outstanding Middlesex player after the Compton Edrich era was Fred Titmus. His best season was 1955, when he took 158 wickets, the highest in a season for the county.

In the sixties, others began to stake their claims for consideration, the best two were Radley and Brearley. Clive Radley was a very sound batsman and a first-class slip fielder, whilst Mike Brearley scored consistently as Russell's opening partner after coming into the side after the Cambridge term.

It was 1971 when Mike Brearley interrupted his academic career to return as captain. He soon lost the services of Russell and Parfitt, but new faces were on the horizon and the side was developing nicely. In the attack, were Mike Selvey, Phil Edmonds and John Emburey, whilst Mike Smith, Clive Radley, Roland Butcher and Graham Barlow were all getting runs.

After finishing as runners-up in both the Gillette and Benson and Hedges Cups in 1975, it all came together the following season, when Middlesex won the Championship.

Graham Barlow had an outstanding year with the bat, scoring 1374 runs in all matches at an average of 49.07, whilst both Brearley and Smith also passed 1300 runs. Perhaps their main strength lay in their bowling with Titmus, Selvey, Edmonds and Jones all topping the 70 wicket mark in all first-class matches.

In 1977, Middlesex shared the Championship with Kent and won the Gillette Cup for the first time. Wayne Daniel played a very significant part in that successful season. Not only was he a great fast bowler, but he was a cricketer who was totally committed to Middlesex's cause. Brearley also had a great belief in Mike Gatting, not always shared by others, but in his first full season, he scored a thousand runs.

Few would dispute that Middlesex were by now the leading county, but of course one has to pay a price for success. In 1978, Brearley, Edmonds and Radley played in all six Tests whilst Emburey made his debut in the last Test against New Zealand.

In 1980, the county signed wicket-keeper Paul Downton from Kent and Vincent van der Bijl, a fast-medium pace bowler from South Africa. It had been expected that Daniel would be in the West Indian party, but he wasn't and that enabled Middlesex to bowl both Daniel and Vincent van der Bijl in harness. Also John Emburey had now emerged as one of the leading off-spinners in world cricket and was supported by Edmonds and Selvey.

Brearley hit the first century of the 1980 season, but the county had to wait until the third match of the summer against Sussex at Lord's to register their first victory. The batting was very solid with Gatting, Barlow, Butcher and Radley all making valuable contributions. The fielding was brilliant and coupled with the strongest county attack with a good balance of pace and spin, went a long way to Middlesex lifting the title.

This was the last year that the 60-over competition was being sponsored by Gillette; Middlesex defeating Surrey in the final by 7 wickets. The man of the match was Mike Brearley with an undefeated 96. The county also reached the semi-final of the Benson and Hedges Cup and finished third in the John Player League – surpassing all other county performances since the inception of the four competitions.

Inevitably the following season was something of an anti-climax. Vincent van der Bijl didn't return and his replacement was Australia's Jeff Thomson. He was injured and only played in six Championship matches. When he did play, against Essex at Lord's, there was a unique event, the entire Middlesex side was made up of eleven Test players.

Due to Test calls, the county had the opportunity to blood a young fast bowler by the name of Norman Cowans. Perhaps the batsman to make the greatest advance that summer was Wilf Slack who was paired to open the innings against Kent with Graham Barlow. They shared an unbeaten stand of 367 in the second innings, a new Middlesex record.

The 1982 season was to be Mike Brearley's last season. There was a great determination that Middlesex should mark his departure with a trophy. They looked as though they were going to win all four, as by mid-June, they had not lost a match in any competition. As it was, the county won the Championship title, due in the main to Brearley's astute leadership and the fine bowling of Wayne Daniel.

Mike Brearley led the county for twelve seasons, the successes coming in the final eight seasons, when Middlesex won four Championships (one shared) and two Gillette Cups.

His successor was Mike Gatting, a different character in every way from Brearley. His approach to captaincy was as uncomplicated as his batting. He made a good start, leading his side to victory against Essex in the Benson and Hedges Cup Final by four runs. The county had to settle for second place in the Championship, after contesting for top spot with Essex all season.

The following season saw Essex retain the Championship, Middlesex finishing third, but the county did win the Nat West Trophy, beating Kent by four wickets. Mike Gatting was in superb form, scoring over 3000 runs in all matches. At Bath, against Somerset, shortly after being left out of the England side, he hit 258 in 276 minutes – the highest score made for the county since Jack Robertson's triple century in 1949.

Middlesex won the title for the fifth time in ten seasons in 1985 and then won the Benson and Hedges Cup for a second time in 1986, beating Kent by two runs.

In 1987, the first time in six years, Middlesex did not win a trophy. Norman Cowans missed most of the season following a hernia operation and it proved to be the last for both Clive Radley and Phil Edmonds. Radley retired after almost quarter of a century as a Middlesex player and Edmonds was not offered another contract, though both players had served the county well.

Middlesex were back in business in 1988, winning the Nat West Trophy and then losing in the final the following year.

In 1990, the county won the Refuge Cup, defeating Derbyshire in the final, but more importantly, won the County Championship in what was a two-horse race with Essex. One of the greatest contributions made to the development of Middlesex's championship-winning side came from Barbadian Desmond Haynes. He not only scored 2346 runs in all matches at an average of 69.00, but was tremendously helpful to the young Middlesex batsmen.

The future of the county looks extremely rosy, with Angus Fraser, probably the best new-ball bowler in England to lead the attack. The county also possess in Brown, Roseberry, Tufnell and Ramprakash, four players who I feel are destined to make a big impact this decade; Tufnell having made his Test debut in Australia during the 1990-91 tour and Ramprakash against the West Indies in 1991.

The county have over the past 128 years had some great players, hopefully this book captures the flavour of some of them!

GUBBY ALLEN

Born: 31 July 1902, Bellevue Hill, Australia
Died: 9 November 1989
Played: 1921–1950

FIRST-CLASS MIDDLESEX RECORDS

Matches	*Innings*	*NO*	*Runs*	*HS*	*Ave*	*100s*
146	210	28	4,667	155	25.64	4

Runs	*Wkts*	*Ave*	*Best*	*5wI*	*Ct*
8,668	420	20.64	10-40	27	56

TEST MATCHES: 25

George Oswald Browning Allen was born at Bellevue Hill in Sydney, Australia and was the nephew of R C Allen who played for Australia in the second Test of 1886-87.

It was in 1908 when Walter Allen and his wife and their young family left Sydney to live in England. He later became Sir Walter Allen, Commandant, Metropolitan Special Constabulary. Right from his schooldays at Summerfields, Oxford, young George showed that he had cricket in the blood. He went to Eton in 1915, where he was coached by both C M Wells (a member of the Middlesex Championship side of 1903) and George Hirst (the great Yorkshire all-rounder).

The first time he played at Lord's was in the game against Harrow in 1919, when he was run out without receiving a ball!

Plum Warner had gone to live in the same Buckinghamshire village and became very friendly with the Allen family. He wanted Gubby for Middlesex and got him. His successful career with Eton was crowned when he made his Middlesex debut in August 1921, as a 19 year old schoolboy. He played against both Somerset and Warwickshire that month, taking a wicket in each match, as Middlesex ran out winners on both occasions. It was a bold move by Frank Mann, though Allen was the outstanding Public Schools fast bowler of the year.

At Cambridge in 1922, he obtained his Blue as a freshman in a strong side, but surprisingly he wasn't elected captain the following season and came down to assist Middlesex earlier than expected.

Unfortunately for Middlesex in those days, he was never able to devote all his time to cricket. There was the Royal Exchange, a silk business in France, Debenhams and a firm of stockbrokers, who were all responsible for depriving Middlesex of his ability – this restriction never allowed him to play for more than half a season. In those early years, he bowled at a very quick pace against Nottinghamshire, taking 6 wickets in 33 balls, finishing with 6 for 1 as Middlesex won by 27 runs.

Allen's matches for Middlesex tended to be against the strongest opposition and as Lancashire had won the Championship for the past three seasons, Haig the Middlesex captain was most insistent that Allen should play against the red-rose county in June 1929. Allen agreed, but couldn't be at Lord's on time, as he had to go into Debenhams first to let them know he was playing cricket. When he arrived at the ground at 11.50 am Lancashire had been batting for twenty minutes and hadn't lost a wicket. He was put on to bowl first change and went on to produce one of the finest pieces of bowling.

At tea, Lancashire were 215 for 4, but collapsed soon afterwards to 241 all out – Allen had taken all 10 wickets. It was done on a plumb pitch (Ernest Tyldesley made 102) against a very strong batting side. He clean bowled eight men and had Hopwood caught behind by Fred Price; McDonald was stumped off a slower, wider ball as he advanced down the track.

His final figures are a Middlesex record and the only time a bowler has taken ten wickets in a county game at Lord's. They were:

0	*M*	*R*	*W*
25.3	10	40	10

Two months later at the Oval, he hit 155 as he and Harry Lee added 319 for the second wicket.

One of the fastest of all Middlesex bowlers, he had the perfect bowling action. He had a rhythmic sideways-on action and always extracted maximum pace from the surface. He aimed his attack on the off stump, often suffering from a lack of match practice and was handicapped by a lack of support when playing for Middlesex, yet on his day, he was able to beat any batsman by sheer pace, combined with accurate length.

When he first started to play first-class cricket, his batting was only a minor consideration, yet by the time he played Test cricket he had become a genuine all-rounder.

He played in 25 tests, eight of them as captain when he took tours to Australia in 1936-37 and the West Indies in 1947-48. On the 1932-33 'bodyline' tour of Australia, he claimed 21 wickets, though he will always be remembered for his refusal to bowl bodyline against Woodfull's men for Douglas Jardine. His highest score with the bat at test level was 122 made against the New Zealanders at Lord's in 1931. In the three Tests against India in 1936, he took 20 wickets for 330 runs at an average of 16.50, with his best ever figures, 7 for 80 at the Oval.

On the 1936-37 tour of Australia, he went out of his way to heal man of the wounds that had been created some for years earlier with our oldest friends. In fact, he made 54 speeches on that Australian tour. His best performance with the ball on that trip was 5 for 35 at Brisbane, as Australia were shot out for 58 in their second innings.

For Middlesex, his best season with the bat was 1924, when he scored 618 runs, whilst the summer of 1936 was his best with the ball, when he took 54 wickets. He only played in nine Championship games that season, but with a top score of 137 v Worcestershire at Lord's, he averaged 50.66.

Also in that game he had match figures of 7 for 74 to complete a good all-round performance.

It was no different after the war, for in 1946 at the age of 44, he took 5 for 26 against Yorkshire, including the wicket of Maurice Leyland for nought. In 1948 at the age of 46, he hit the highest score of his career, 180 in a match outside the county programme. Even in 1949, when Middlesex were severely weakened by Test calls, he came into the side and performed well. He hit 98 against Worcestershire, when Jack Robertson hit his triple hundred and 91 against Somerset as well as taking the first three wickets to fall in the Somerset innings. He ended the season with 13 cheap wickets and 199 runs from four innings to finish top of the bowling averages and second in the batting averages!

He played his last match in August 1950 against Somerset at Weston-super-Mare.

He was the youngest by nine years when elected to the MCC Committee – with Billy Griffith he helped form the Cricket Council which led to the establishment of the TCCB and NCA. He had been Chairman of the test selectors from 1955 to 1961 – a most successful period; they selected on class rather than averages. He was MCC President in 1963-64, its treasurer from 1964 to 1976 and then became one of its Trustees.

On his 80th birthday, his services to the game were honoured by the MCC with a dinner in the Long Room at Lord's. The only other player to have this honour bestowed upon them was Sir Pelham Warner.

He was awarded the Territorial Decoration in 1945, following outstanding service during the war, appointed CBE in 1962 and was knighted for his services to cricket in 1986. He must surely rank alongside W G Grace, Lord Harris and Sir Pelham Warner as one of crickets most powerful influences.

Towards the end of his life, he needed a stick to walk the short distance from his house to Lord's after having undergone six hip replacement operations.

Shortly before his death, it was announced that Q Stand was being renamed The Allen Stand – his name living on at Lord's forever, a great tribute to a famous England cricketer and captain who never made either 1000 runs or took 100 wickets in a season.

GRAHAM BARLOW

Born: 23 March 1950, Folkestone
Played: 1969–1986

FIRST-CLASS MIDDLESEX RECORDS

Matches	*Innings*	*NO*	*Runs*	*HS*	*Ave*	*100s*
238	385	57	11640	177	35.48	23

Runs	*Wkts*	*Ave*	*Best*	*5wI*	*Ct*
66	3	22.0	1-6	0	130

TEST MATCHES: 3

Graham Barlow was not so much bred into cricket as recruited into it. His father had never played the game and wasn't attracted until Graham played for Ealing Grammar School, showing a natural ability that made him a player of great promise.

First came the chance to play for Middlesex Schools and when he went on tour with them to Pakistan in 1968, he still managed to average over 50 with the bat, even after dislocating a knee and receiving a black eye! Then there came invitations from English and MCC Schools and at the end of the season, he was presented with the Best Schoolboy Fielder award by John Arlott.

As soon as he left school in 1969, Middlesex took him on the staff. He made his debut in the game against Lancashire and after defending stoutly for over two hours in the second innings, he was bowled off the very last ball of the match, giving Lancashire victory by 14 runs. However, he was to gain his revenge against the red-rose county in the years to come.

Wisely, Middlesex insisted on Barlow extending his qualifications to ensure his future. So in 1970, he went to Loughborough to study P.E. for three years. For a while though, cricket had to take a back seat as he concentrated on athletics and rugby. He represented the College in sprints and the long jump in 1972 and won a place at centre in the England Under-23 XV at Kendal. It's probably his experiences on the rugby field that accounted for his heroic plunges on the various outfields of the country.

His first full season of county cricket was 1976 and coincided with Middlesex winning the Championship. Prior to the 1976 season, he had scored plenty of runs on a brief pre-season visit to Germany. It was this new found belief in his ability which enabled him to have a most successful season. He began with 85 against Kent and then one consistent effort followed another. He hit only two centuries in the championship–160 not out against Derbyshire at Lord's and 140 against Essex at Chelmsford, but ended the season with an aggregate of 1478 runs at an average of 49. This total number of runs was more than he'd scored previously in his career and was more than double his score in 1975. He also made his first Sunday League hundred, 104 against Somerset at Bath. He ended the season with distinction, being selected for a one-day international against the West Indies at Scarborough, helping himself to 80 not out. This earned him a place on the winter tour.

Sadly, he just failed to make the demanding transition to Test level and on his three appearances for England, he did nothing of note with the bat, though he impressed with some brilliant work in the field. In fact, he has the embarrassing Test average of 4.25, yet in 1977 he topped the averages on England's tour of India, Sri Lanka and Australia.

On the domestic front, Northamptonshire suffered at the hands of Barlow's bat in the 1977 season. He hit 129 at Northampton in the Benson and Hedges Cup and 101 not out at Lord's in the John Player League.

Graham Barlow was a self-made batsman. He wasn't the most stylish of left-handers, relying essentially on his natural ability. His method was forceful, the thrusting out of his right leg as he drove the ball through the covers was a rousing sight on the Lord's ground. Barlow though possessed a wide array of strokes and scored consistently at county level. In fact, it is quite remarkable to note that the county's Championship successes in the period 1976-85 coincided with consistent and aggressive contributions from Graham Barlow.

He had never really settled into a position in the batting line-up until the 1981 season, when the experimental opening partnership of Barlow and Wilf Slack blossomed. In the second innings of the match against Kent he and Slack put on an unbeaten stand of 367 in 247 minutes. Barlow hit 174 (four sixes and 16 fours) yet later that season, he hit the highest score of his career, 177 against Lancashire at Southport in an innings I remember well. It was this ability to open the innings, scoring at a brisk rate, that went a long way in helping Middlesex to their Championship successes, blending well with the more cautious Slack.

Barlow was a model professional, always striving for perfection with his fielding and offering great encouragement to the bowlers.

In 1984, he hit a magnificent 158 against Lancashire at Lord's in the Nat West trophy, to revenge once more the county that he'd made his debut against. It was around this time that he began to be immobilised by an old hip injury. He even saw a faith healer about the problem and strapped a special stone to his leg at nights. This was also his benefit season, yet two years later, he'd played his last game for Middlesex.

In the opening match of the 1986 season, he hit 18 and 52 not out against Derbyshire. He missed the next two matches with a back injury, returning to hit 107 against Sussex. The next match against Surrey, saw him score 12 and turned out to be his last match. The back problem was so severe that it caused his retirement from the first-class game. His departure was the first sign that the great team Middlesex had, was beginning to break up.

Graham Barlow was a dependable and whole-hearted cricketer, a tower of strength to the Middlesex side.

DON BENNETT

Born: 18 December 1933, Wakefield, Yorkshire
Played: 1950–1968

FIRST-CLASS MIDDLESEX RECORDS

Matches	*Innings*	*NO*	*Runs*	*HS*	*Ave*	*100s*
392	590	120	10274	117*	21.85	4

Runs	*Wkts*	*Ave*	*Best*	*5wI*	*Ct*
19790	748	26.45	7-47	22	156

TEST MATCHES: 0

Though he was born in Wakefield, Yorkshire, Don Bennett had lived in Middlesex since 1940. In the early part of 1950, his family moved to live in Staffordshire, but Middlesex offered him a contract in order that he could continue his academic studies at Ashford County Grammar School and thus retain his residential qualification for the County.

A fast-medium bowler with an orthodox bowling action, he made his Middlesex debut in 1950 at the age of 16.

As a schoolboy, Bennett had been earmarked as a future England all-rounder, yet he fell between two stools, batting too low down in the order.

By the time he had reached 19, he had such a consistent season with the bat that even though his top score was only 66, he topped 1000 runs and averaged almost 30. He was also taking around 40 wickets per season and so he was a valuable member of the Middlesex side, though he could only be used sparingly.

By 1952, Middlesex had the more regular services of Don Bennett. He had been invalided out of the RAF with defective hearing. With Jack Hearne, Bennett worked hard to improve his batting, though his fast-medium bowling never quite reached the heights that had been anticipated.

In 1953, he batted with great consistency and was one of the most brilliant fielders in the country. On the bowling front, he showed great signs of improvement, though it was only on rare occasions that he was given the new ball.

He hit four hundreds in his career, his maiden century coming in 1954 against his native Yorkshire at Lord's – it was an innings that rather surprisingly gave Middlesex the first innings points.

In 1956, he began to do himself justice as a bowler. He stepped up to replace Alan Moss with the new ball, Moss tearing a stomach muscle.

He was continuing to make useful contributions with the bat and shared in two useful partnerships with wicket-keeper John Murray. In 1961, they added 182 for the seventh wicket against Glamorgan at Lord's and three years later they added an undefeated 220 also for the seventh wicket against Yorkshire at Headingley.

By 1965 and only 31, he was beginning to tail off, though he did go on to play for a further three years. A career total of 10,274 runs and 748 wickets wasn't really worthy of a player who had so much ability.

He played his last game for the county in 1968 after probably being Middlesex's most successful bowler in the early years of the one-day competitions. It is a pity he wasn't starting his career at that time for I'm sure he would have excelled in the one-day game.

Now an invaluable member of the Middlesex staff, his wisdom and expertise are still being used on the coaching side to great advantage.

BERNARD BOSANQUET

Born: 13 October 1877
Died: 12 October 1936
Played: 1898–1919

FIRST-CLASS MIDDLESEX RECORDS

Matches	*Innings*	*NO*	*Runs*	*HS*	*Ave*	*100s*
123	200	13	6593	179	35.26	13

Runs	*Wkts*	*Ave*	*Best*	*5wI*	*Ct*
7271	268	27.13	8-53	19	91

TEST MATCHES: 7

Born on 13 October 1877, Bernard Bosanquet was sent to Eton, where he profited from the coaching of Surrey professionals, William Brockwell and Maurice Read. After getting his place in the XI, he hit 120 against Harrow in 1896, but it wasn't sufficient to secure a Blue in his first year at Oriel College, Oxford.

He received his Blue in his second year from F H E Cunliffe and though he played against Cambridge three times, he did nothing exceptional. He played soccer for his college and represented the University at Hammer Throwing and Billiards. He did find time to tour Ireland twice with I Zingari, the United States in 1898 with Plum Warner and again the following year with Ranji.

In 1897, he was playing 'twisti-twosti'– where the object was to spin a tennis ball past your opponent who was seated at the other end of a table. Bosanquet's over-the-wrist action sent the ball rather puzzlingly bouncing from his opponents right side to his left. Within two years, he had become the 'star-turn' at the nets during the intervals of Oxford University's matches. His demonstrations of reverse spin with a cricket ball surprised a few visiting county batsmen.

He made his Middlesex debut in 1898, playing in just one match. He took his first wicket for the county the following season in the match against Surrey when he clean bowled Bobby Abel.

At the turn of the century, the family moved to Uxbridge; he joined the local club and played up to the outbreak of the War. There were quite a few clubs who shared his services with Middlesex, these included I Zingari, Eton Ramblers, Free Foresters, Incogniti and numerous country-house teams.

Bosanquet experimented further with his delivery in minor matches, until he gathered enough nerve to try it in a county game. His first victim with his new invention was Sam Coe of Leicestershire who was stumped at Lord's for 98, from a ball that bounced four times. This was also one of the matches in which Bosanquet scored two centuries, 136 and 139. His first hundred came out of a stand of 120 after he'd been dropped at both 0 and 99. The great Nottinghamshire batsman, William Gunn was stumped 10 yards down the wicket it was reported the following month!

In the 1925 Wisden, Bosanquet wrote: 'It took any amount of perseverance, but for a year or two the results were more than worth it, for in addition to adding to the merriment of the cricketing world, I found that batsmen who used to grin at the sight of me and grasp their bat firmly by the long handle began to show a marked preference for the other end!' Perhaps the first county side to feel this way were Sussex, when playing Oxford, Bosanquet took 9 for 31 (15 for 65 in the match) his match analysis remains the record for Oxbridge.

Bernard Bosanquet brought the ball over from a great height so that the flight as well as the uncertain break mystified batsmen until the entire team became demoralised. As a batsman, he was dashing stiff-armed, yet powerful and with a good eye.

In 1901-02, he took a hat-trick for R A Bennett's XI against Barbados at Bridgetown. In 1902, R O Schwarz, a Richmond and England rugby player, joined Middlesex for an unsuccessful season. It was in the nets at both Uxbridge and Lord's that he became the originator's one and only pupil. Schwarz then took a post as secretary to the South African tycoon, Sir Abe Bailey and after little success with the 'googly' he returned to England in 1904, heading the averages with 96 wickets at 14.81 each.

In the winter of 1902-03, Bosanquet toured New Zealand and Australia with a team captained by Pelham Warner, after Lord Hawke had withdrawn. After losing to both Victoria and South Australia and only managing a draw with New South Wales (he scored 114 in under 90 minutes), England entered the first Test with a little trepidation! On a perfect Sydney wicket, Bosanquet took 6 for 153, including Trumper who lost his middle stump to Bosanquet's googly.

He was chosen to tour Australia again in 1903-04 with the MCC though his selection caused quite an outburst, with accusations that Plum Warner must have insisted on the inclusion of his Oxford and Middlesex colleague!

Prior to the first Test, he scored 99 in a minor match before being run out, 79 against Victoria and 4 for 60 against New South Wales. In the Test, he took three important wickets for 152 and though England won, he lost his place for the next. He returned for the third Test to take 3 for 95 and 4 for

73, but Australia won the match with both Gregory and Trumper hitting hundreds. Bosanquet then hit two fine attacking hundreds against Tasmania and New South Wales, the latter coming in only 75 minutes and took 6 for 45 in their second innings. In the fourth Test, Australia needed 329 to win and Bosanquet (nicknamed 'Elsie' by the inhabitants of the Hill because of his colourful sweater) took 6 for 51, (5 for 12 at one period) as England won back the Ashes.

His best season was 1904 when he scored 1405 runs and took 132 wickets. He indulged in some tremendous hitting that summer; 141 v Yorkshire at Sheffield; 110 v South Africa in a tied game; 126 in 115 minutes v Surrey at the Oval and 145 at the same ground playing for the Gentlemen against the Players. Also that summer, he took 9 for 107 against the South African tourists when playing at Lord's for the MCC

In 1905, against the Australians in the first Test at Trent Bridge, Jackson's declarations set the men from 'Down Under' 402 to win in five hours. Bosanquet took the first five wickets to fall and ended the match with 8 for 107 from 32.4 overs to give England victory by 213 runs. He played in the next two Tests and was then dropped from MacLaren's side and never used the 'googly' again in first-class cricket.

Probably Bosanquet's finest game was for Middlesex in their match against Sussex at Lord's just before his superb performance in the 1905 Trent Bridge Test. He scored 103 at a run a minute and then in the second innings, he hit an unbeaten hundred in an hour and a quarter. Sussex needed 427 to win and were dismissed for 102, Bosanquet taking 8 for 53, for a match return of 11 for 128, thus completing one of the most remarkable all-round performances in the history of the game. Not surprisingly, he was a Wisden Cricketer of the Year.

From 1906 onwards, he scored plenty of runs for Middlesex, but the bowling was done by others. He had one more good season in 1908, when he headed the national batting averages. He averaged 50.80 in the nine games he played, including a century in 95 minutes against Lancashire – it was equal to anything seen at Lord's said one report. He also hit an astonishing century in just 25 minutes, playing for Uxbridge against the MCC. He represented the Rest of England in that summer of 1908 against Surrey at the Oval scoring 214 in 195 minutes.

He continued to play on and off until 1919, but his career was all too short, becoming interrupted by business. During the First World War, he served in the Kite Balloon section of the Royal Flying Corps.

Six years after retiring from first-class cricket with Middlesex, he scored a 75 minute century for the Gentlemen at Scarborough against a Players side that contained Sid Barnes.

The father of the now deceased ITN newsreader Reginald, he had with his back-of-the-hand delivery often called a 'Bosie', advanced cricket more than anything since the introduction of overarm bowling.

Probably the most effective amateur of his day, he died in 1936 at Wykehurst Farm, Ewhurst, Surrey a day short of his sixtieth birthday.

MIKE BREARLEY

Born: 28 April 1942, Harrow
Played: 1961–1983

FIRST-CLASS MIDDLESEX RECORDS

Matches	*Innings*	*NO*	*Runs*	*HS*	*Ave*	*100s*
291	485	68	15985	173*	38.33	29

Runs	*Wkts*	*Ave*	*Best*	*5wI*	*Ct*	*St*
119	1	119.00	1-6	0	210	1

TEST MATCHES: 39

Born in 1942 in Harrow, Mike Brearley was part of a games playing and particularly cricket-playing family (his father had played for both Yorkshire and Middlesex). He attended the City of London School, from where he won a scholarship to Cambridge to read Classics and Philosophy. He achieved a high academic distinction at Cambridge, taking a 1st in Classics and a good 2nd in Moral Sciences; in addition, he scored 4310 runs in his four years – more than anyone else before or since. He was captain for two of his four years at Fenners and hit ten centuries. He created something of a stir by bowling underarm against Oxford University!

He first played for Middlesex in 1961 as John Murray's deputy, the Middlesex wicket-keeper played for England in the fourth Test. Brearley played against Derbyshire at Lord's and Hampshire at Portsmouth, scoring just 42 runs and taking six catches.

In his first full season, he scored 1222 first-class runs at an average of 35.94. He was in his early days a very good wicket-keeper, though after his days at Cambridge, he seldom had the chance to do so. He came into the side after the Cambridge term and scored consistently as Russell's opening partner.

His best season with the bat was 1964 when he scored 2178 first-class runs at an average of 44.44 and was elected Best Young Cricketer of the Year by the Cricket Writers' Club. He toured South Africa with the MCC in 1964-65, though with little success. He didn't play in 1966 and 1967, but re-appeared in the latter half of each season between 1968 and 1970.

He led an MCC Under-25 team to Pakistan in 1966-67, taking all the honours both off and on the field. It was on this tour that he achieved his highest ever first-class score of 312 not out, made on the first day of the match against North Zone at Peshawar.

After the 1970 season, the Middlesex Committee tried to persuade Brearley to return to the fold. However, he wasn't interested in just a playing capacity and so the captaincy was added as a further incentive – this he accepted. He liked a challenge and certainly wouldn't have returned to the county in any other guise.

When he became captain in 1971, he came with a very successful record for both Cambridge and for the MCC under-25's in Pakistan, yet his record for Middlesex was fairly undistinguished. He hadn't scored a thousand runs or hit a century for the county and wasn't to do either until 1973.

Right from the outset of Brearley's reign as captain, the county began to play adventurous and forthright cricket–there was an improvement in results, but no instant success. The county were top of the Championship Table until August when Brearley was injured and had to settle for sixth place.

His first Championship hundred came in the last county match at Lord's in 1973 when Yorkshire were the opponents, when he scored 134 not out. In the return game at Bradford (the last match of the season) he almost repeated the feat, but was dismissed for 83.

He hit his highest first-class score for Middlesex 173 not out against Glamorgan at Cardiff in 1974, following it with an unbeaten 163 against Yorkshire in the next match. He also hit 124 not out against Buckinghamshire at Lord's in a Gillette Cup fixture.

Though his batting never quite fulfilled its early promise, one of his assets was that he could bat anywhere in the order, though he was successful eventually as an opening batsman. In 1975, he scored 1656 runs at an average of 53.41 to finish as the second Englishman in the national batting averages.

In the opening County Championship match of the 1976 season, he made 153 against Kent at Lord's and carried his bat for 128 against Hampshire in the next match, though Middlesex were well beaten. Later in the season, the England selectors omitted him from the Test side, but he responded with 106 v Sussex on a difficult pitch. The county went on to win the Championship and were the only county side to beat the West Indian tourists – for Mike Brearley it was the start of a run of success that can usually only be found in Boy's Own! At the end of the season, he was named as one of Wisden's Cricketers of the Year.'

In 1976-77 he was made vice-captain to Tony Greig on the Indian tour (with only 2 Test appearances behind him). It was on this tour that he hit his best Test score, 91 at Bombay. Then the following summer, he was made captain of England when the extent of Greig's involvement with Kerry Packer became known. E M Wellings in his book states the view of many when it was thought he might become a Test batsman and captain – that was rating him too highly!

Mike Brearley was an outstanding captain; his tactical acumen and training in philosophy made him a great leader of cricketers. He was a great communicator, establishing a rapport with each team member, be it at county or Test level.

He was only the second captain after Sir Len Hutton to regain and then successfully defend the Ashes. He was the first England captain to lead his country to five wins in an Ashes rubber. He was the first captain to gain 11 victories against Australia, equalling Don Bradman's Australian record against England. He captained England on 31 occasions, winning 17 and losing 4.

In 1977, Middlesex won the Gillette Cup and had a half-share in the

County Championship. Though playing in only 11 Championship matches because of Test calls, he scored 953 runs (Average 59.56) to top the Middlesex averages.

The following year he amassed £31,000 from his benefit and was awarded the OBE in the New Year honours list.

By 1980, he had relinquished the England captaincy and was the first Middlesex player to hit a Championship century, 134 not out v Lancashire in the second match of the season. At Cardiff he hit a magnificent 124 not out against Glamorgan and during the course of the season, he hit centuries in the other two one-day competitions, 100 not out v Surrey in the Benson and Hedges Cup and 109 not out v Somerset in the John Player League. In the 1980 Gillette Cup Final, he won the Man of the Match Award with a commanding innings of 96.

In 1981, with England 1-0 down to Australia, he was recalled to lead the national side. He rallied the side round to a magnificent 3-1 victory.

There was a determination throughout the Middlesex camp in 1982, that the side should mark Mike Brearley's last season with a trophy. In fact, they didn't lose a match in any competition until mid-June. In his last match in 1982, he hit the winning run at Worcester to lead Middlesex to the County Championship – a fitting testimony to his marvellous career in cricket with Cambridge, Middlesex and England.

The tributes poured in; Wisden commenting: 'So Brearley departed after a dozen seasons of captaincy, festooned with honours at Test and county level.'– He also restored purposeful cricket to Lord's, while winning four Championships (one shared) and two Gillette Cups.

He has often been described as a ruthless captain, but then many of the great leaders have had this approach and there is no doubt that Mike Brearley achieved all the success he strove for.

A man of many talents, he has since retiring from the leadership concentrated on psychotherapy, teaching and writing.

Vyell Walker

Isaac Walker

George Burton

Tim O'Brien

Gregor MacGregor

Andrew Stoddart

John Rawlin bowling at Lord's in 1892

Jack T Hearne

Albert Trott

Pelham Warner

Bernard Bosanquet

Frank Tarrant

Patsy Hendren

John W Hearne

Frank Mann

Harry Lee

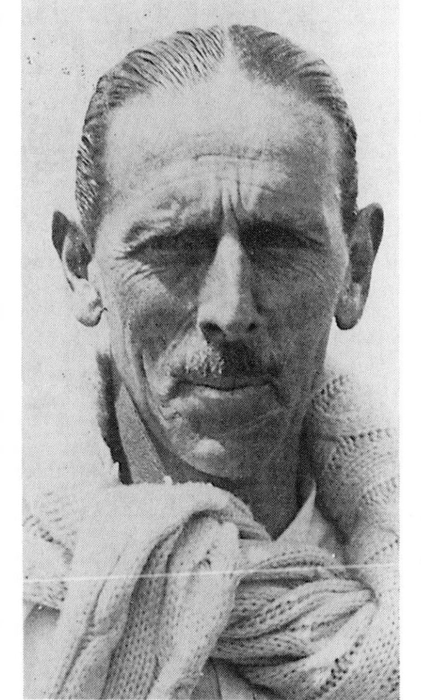

Nigel Haig

Greville Stevens

Gubby Allen

Jack Durston

Walter Robins

Fred Price

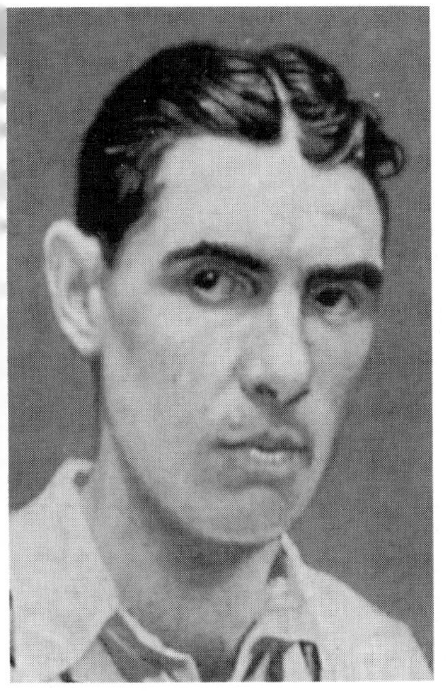

Jim Sims

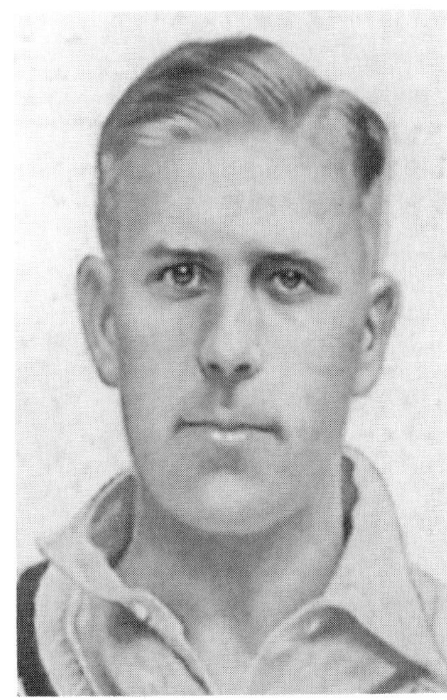

Jim Smith

Ian Peebles

Jack Young

Denis Compton

SYD BROWN

Born: 8 December 1917, Eltham
Died: 28 December 1987
Played: 1937–1955

FIRST-CLASS MIDDLESEX RECORDS

Matches	*Innings*	*NO*	*Runs*	*HS*	*Ave*	*100s*
313	549	39	15050	232*	29.51	20

Runs	*Wkts*	*Ave*	*Best*	*5wI*	*Ct*
80	3	26.67	2-19	0	146

TEST MATCHES: 0

Syd Brown made his Middlesex debut in 1937 against Oxford University at The Parks, opening the batting with E W Swanton, who was also making his first-class debut. At the end of the 1937 season, Middlesex were approached by Kent in an attempt to get the registration of Syd Brown, who because he'd been born in Eltham had a birth qualification. Middlesex refused to let Brown go and he held down a regular place in the two years leading up to the war.

He was the first young batsman to be tried as Edrich's opening partner, scoring his first hundred against Lancashire at Old Trafford. However, he didn't in those two years really fulfil the promise he'd shown when making high scores in the 2nd XI; he seemed a little slow on his feet and rather stereotyped in his stroke play, yet he certainly made great strides after the war.

A top-class batsman in the period immediately after the hostilities, he was primarily a cutter, though he could also hook the ball that was short of a length. He was never given a chance to play for England and was surely a more sensible choice than some who represented their country between 1946 and 1951.

By 1946, he had become a very efficient opener, helping Jack Robertson put up over 100 for the first wicket on six occasions Brown and Robertson were a magnificent opening pair. They set a new Middlesex record in 1947, as they added over 100 for the first wicket on nine occasions.

He carried his bat for 150 against Derbyshire as Middlesex won by 212 runs. He and Robertson attacked the bowling – against Essex, they put on 169 together in 78 minutes. Against Northamptonshire, he scored 98, failing by two runs to join Robertson, Edrich and Compton as centurions and thus equal the club's unique record of having all first four batsmen passing the century mark. He scored 130 as he and Jack Robertson added 222 for the first wicket against Yorkshire. When the same pair added 310 in the next match against Nottinghamshire at Lord's, it was a Middlesex record for the first wicket (since twice beaten); Syd Brown scored 155 (a six and 16 fours).

A brave batsman, he was hit in the face by a ball from Wilf Wooller of Glamorgan on a wicket that gave every encouragement to the bowler and had to be carried off on a stretcher. Middlesex were chasing 201 to win and at 102 for 5, Syd Brown returned and batted bravely helping Alec Thompson add 71 as Middlesex won by three wickets.

He ended the 1947 season with 1700 runs at 40.00 (over 2000 runs in all matches).

He carried his bat magnificently the following season as Middlesex were bowled out for a total of 153 by Cambridge University, scoring 96 not out.

In 1949, he made his first score of 200 in county cricket against Kent at Canterbury. His innings contained 21 fours and was as Wisden put it 'an innings of hard drives, sure pulls and neat late cuts' Brown ending the season with 1636 runs. In 1950, he scored 1089 runs at an average of 28.65 with a top score of 142. The following summer, he scored 232 not out against Somerset at Lord's and shared in two long stands – 199 for the first wicket with Robertson and 198 with Dewes for the third wicket. Against Hampshire, he scored 194 as he and Robertson put on 232 in just over three hours.

He was perhaps a little vulnerable to the ball that dipped into him, but he was an exciting batsman to watch. He shared in two long stands with Bill Edrich – 267 against Oxford University at The Parks in 1952 for the third wicket and then 324 against Warwickshire at Edgbaston in 1954 for the second wicket.

Syd Brown was one of the finest outfielders in county cricket – of medium height and chunky build, he could get down to the ball and throw it in, all in one movement, whilst running at full speed.

E M Wellings in his book refers to a catch he witnessed by Brown against Surrey; running at full speed, he took the ball at full stretch some three yards inside the boundary, before his impetus carried him well over the boundary – nowadays of course, the batsman would have been credited with a six.

Playing his last match in 1955, he scored 15050 runs for Middlesex at an average of 29.50 with 20 centuries.

GEORGE BURTON

Born: Hampstead, 1 May 1851
Died: 7 May 1930
Played: 1881–1893

FIRST-CLASS MIDDLESEX RECORDS

Matches	*Innings*	*NO*	*Runs*	*HS*	*Ave*	*100s*
111	176	54	946	34	7.75	0

Runs	*Wkts*	*Ave*	*Best*	*5wI*	*Ct*
9081	529	17.17	10-59	43	90

TEST MATCHES: 0

George Burton was a slow right-handed bowler who made his debut for Middlesex in 1881 at the age of thirty. He was a coachsmith by trade and even on the days that he played for Middlesex, he would put in several hours' work before entering the field of play.

His first match was against Surrey at Lord's and with only his second delivery, he dismissed Harry Jupp. In Surrey's second innings, he took 5 for 20, including the wicket of Surrey captain John Shuter first ball.

In 1886, when Middlesex played the Australians at Lord's, Burton bowled over 100 overs in the match and ended with match figures of 14 for 192. He took 6 for 56 in Australia's second innings as the men from Down Under scraped home by one wicket amid great excitement.

In his most successful season, 1888, he began with ten wickets against Yorkshire at Lord's and then took nine against Lancashire, also at home. He took eleven in the next match, as Middlesex beat rivals Nottinghamshire by an innings and 55 runs. When Middlesex played the Australians on a terrible wicket, Burton had match figures of 8 for 51, including 6 for 39 in the Australians' first innings.

In that 1888 season, Burton took all ten Surrey wickets for 59 at the Oval. Four of his victims were caught by Robertson at short slip and he ended the innings with a bowling analysis of:

Overs	*Maidens*	*Runs*	*Wkts*
52.3	25	59	10

When Surrey went in to bat for a second time, they only needed 52 to win. They lost seven wickets in the process, Burton following his ten wicket haul with 3 for 19.

The following match was at Sheffield against Yorkshire. The white-rose county were dismissed for 112, Burton taking 8 for 48, and 122 with Burton once again snapping up eight wickets for 66 runs. His match analysis of 16 for 114 was equalled for Middlesex ten years later by J T Hearne in the match against Lancashire, but they have never been bettered and Burton still shares the County record. He always seemed to bowl well against

Yorkshire at Lord's, producing figures of 7 for 20 and 7 for 18 in successive matches in the late 1880s.

He ended that 1888 season with 79 championship wickets at the remarkable cost of 12.20 runs each. When one considers the lack of support given to him, his record was exceptionally good. If he'd had more support throughout his career, then Middlesex would have performed better than they did.

He bowled well for the next two seasons, without reaching the same heights as 1888. He then came back in 1893 to play in just one game, appropriately against Yorkshire. He failed to take a wicket in the fifteen overs that he bowled, but he hit six runs and caught Wainwright. He played for ten seasons in the Middlesex side, taking 504 wickets at a cost of 16.83.

Burton was a member of the MCC ground staff and in 1894 against Oxford City, he once again took all ten wickets in an innings. He had two benefits, the first being in 1892 when Middlesex played Surrey and the second in 1905 when Middlesex entertained Somerset. On his retirement from the first-class game, he scored for Middlesex and was also coach at Mill Hill School. He was also honorary secretary to the Cricketers' Fund Friendly Society right up to his death on 7 May 1930 at the age of 79.

George Burton bowled for the county at a time when they were in need of a regular wicket-keeper of good class. His success was a triumph for the accuracy and endeavour that he put into his bowling.

ROLAND BUTCHER

Born 14 October 1953, East Point, Barbados
Played: 1974–1990

FIRST-CLASS MIDDLESEX RECORDS

Matches	*Innings*	*NO*	*Runs*	*HS*	*Ave*	*100s*
237	373	35	10677	197	31.58	17

Runs	*Wkts*	*Ave*	*Best*	*5wI*	*Ct*
159	4	39.75	2-37	0	256

TEST MATCHES: 3

Roland Butcher was born at East Point, St Philip on the island of Barbados, the eldest son of a carpenter. He came to England with his parents in 1967, as the family searched for better opportunities than were available in the depressed Caribbean.

They settled in the new town of Stevenage, Roland's father being employed as an engineer. Roland graduated to the Middlesex side through the Hertfordshire School sides, where even then the talent and flair associated with Caribbean youngsters was evident.

He was on the Lord's ground staff for two years, but prior to this in 1969, he had played for the Gloucestershire 2nd XI. A keen footballer, he has also played at semi-professional level for both Biggleswade and Stevenage.

He joined Middlesex in 1972 and made his debut two years later, but he had to wait until 1978 for his first century and a further year for his county cap. He was never sure of his place, threatening brilliance one-day and looking a complete novice the next.

Against Hampshire in 1980, he hit what was at the time, the highest score of his career, 153 not out (nine sixes and eight fours) as Middlesex won a thrilling victory at Lord's. He followed this with a brilliant 179 against Yorkshire at Scarborough (eight sixes and 21 fours) in under three hours. In the Gillette Cup Final of 1980, against Surrey, he hit an unbeaten 50 to steer Middlesex home by 7 wickets. His 50 came off 41 balls, though it was Brearley with 96 not out who was named Man-of -the-Match.

During the 1980 season he was selected to play for England in the one-day international matches late in the season. He hit a 35-ball fifty against the Australians, thus earning him selection for the 1980-81 Caribbean tour. He was the first black West Indian to play for England, making his Test debut at Kensington Oval in his native Barbados on 14th March 1981.

Butcher realized that to play for England would safeguard his Middlesex career. If he'd played for the West Indies, his position with the county may have been in jeopardy, for the sake of his family's security, it was an opportunity he could not refuse. He was though , among the quietest of the Middlesex players, the least exuberant of West Indians.

He has occasionally deputised as an emergency wicket-keeper, but was really an outstanding fielder with a tremendous throwing arm. Against Australia at Lord's in 1981, he took five catches in an innings. In 1982 he hit the highest score of his career, 197 against Yorkshire at Lord's.

In 1983, he suffered terrible facial injury after being hit in the face by a rising delivery from Leicestershire's George Ferris and was forced to miss the latter half of the season; his loss being deeply felt by the Middlesex side.

As a batsman, he was very attractive to watch, a stroke-maker, often scoring a match-winning hundred. One of these came in a John Player League match against Gloucestershire at Lord's when he hit a brilliant 100 not out. He could be a decisive factor in any county championship match and usually three or four times in a season, he would play an innings that would win a match.

A devout member of the Anglican Church, he works for the Inter-Action group, whose purpose is to bring sport to the disabled and under-privileged young of London.

Although dogged by injuries in 1989 (his only century was 126 against surrey) his benefit year raised £173,000.

He originally agreed to join the unofficial England tour to South Africa in 1989-90, but withdrew from the ill-fated tour after receiving telephone calls and following resignations from his benefit committee. He spent the 1990 season with the 2nd XI, not playing a championship game. The cousin of Basil Butcher (Guyana and West Indies) he has been the most consistent of Middlesex batsmen, yet his contribution to the county's cricket is immeasurable.

DENIS COMPTON

Born: 23 May 1918, Hendon
Played: 1936–1958

FIRST-CLASS MIDDLESEX RECORDS

Matches	*Innings*	*NO*	*Runs*	*HS*	*Ave*	*100s*
296	458	49	21781	252*	49.96	67

Runs	*Wkts*	*Ave*	*Best*	*5wI*	*Ct*
14124	477	29.61	6-63	16	264

TEST MATCHES: 78

Denis Compton made his first appearance at Lords at the age of 13, when he captained the London Elementary Schools against Mr C F Tufnell's Public Schools XI. He scored 114 and impressed Plum Warner so much, that Plum asked Denis' parents if he could join the ground staff there and then. Dad was in full agreement, but Mum of course, was worried about Denis' employment during the winter months. However everything turned out right when Herbert Chapman, manager of Arsenal offered Denis a job on the Highbury staff. Denis joined the Lord's staff a few weeks short of his 15th birthday.

When he first came into the Middlesex XI at the age of 18, he was a slow left-arm bowler with an easy action, spinning from leg. However, Middlesex had plenty of bowlers and so he was only used as an occasional bowler who was brought on to break partnerships. It was clear though, that he was a natural games player, who had the eye of an hawk and an instinctive gift of balance.

He made his Middlesex debut in 1936 against Sussex at Lord's. Going in at No 11, he scored 14, thus enabling Middlesex to gain a narrow lead on the first innings. It may have only seemed a modest start, yet it impressed those that mattered. Later in the season, he hit his first hundred in the match against Northamptonshire. When Ian Peebles joined Compton, the Middlesex score stood at 390 for 9 with Compton on 44. The last wicket pair added 74 of which 56 were scored by Compton. He ended the season with 1004 runs, setting a record by being the youngest player to score 1000 runs in his first season. He was described by Warner as the best young batsman to appear since Wally Hammond.

In 1937, he almost doubled his first season's aggregate and raised his average to 47. Against Gloucestershire at Lords he hit a superb century as the West Country sides fine array of bowlers went to work on a turning wicket.

The following season, despite being only 20, he displayed a maturity and knowledge of the game beyond his years. Against Essex in a game of twisting fortunes, Middlesex were left to make 241 against the leg breaks of Peter Smith. Compton batted gallantly (in fact, 16 of his first 18 runs came in boundaries) but by the time he was joined by last man Baxter, Middlesex still required 24 runs to win. The Number 11 only faced a handful of deliveries, scoring 1, as Compton steered his side to victory.

In 1938, he made the first of his 17 Test centuries, 102 in the match against Australia, becoming the youngest Englishman to score a hundred in these contests.

The 1939 season saw him hit his first double century, an unbeaten 214 against Derbyshire at Lord's and 120 for England against the West Indies in a glorious partnership with Len Hutton. Against Essex he scored 181 – He and Gray adding 81 for the last wicket, with Gray contributing only a single!

In 1938-39, he damaged his knee in a collision with the Charlton Athletic goalkeeper and had a cartilage operation the following season. He was an exciting outside left and a wartime soccer international, going on to gain League and FA Cup winners' medals with Arsenal.

When cricket resumed after the war, Compton ended the 1945 season with 2042 runs at an average of 65.87 with nine centuries. He hit 202 against Cambridge at Fenners and his highest score of the season, 235 against Surrey in 4 hours 40 minutes. Against Lancashire at Old Trafford, he hit 124 and 100, the only time he hit a century in each innings of a match.

Like all great players, Denis used his feet and he was never happier than when gaily trotting down the track to some unfortunate spinner. He was probably the greatest improviser the game of cricket has ever seen. He could change his mind three or four times between the ball being delivered and him hitting it. He possessed all the classical strokes and could be perfectly orthodox, but often he didn't pick a stroke until the last possible moment, which meant that he would get into all sorts of ungainly contortions when he put bat to ball.

Denis though, was more than a great batsman, he was an entertainer and one of the biggest box office draws ever to have played the game and like all entertainers, he thrived on situations and a large audiences.

No cricketer, save possibly Botham, has ever been more of a schoolboy's hero than Denis Compton.

The golden year for the golden boy was 1947 when he scored more runs and made more centuries than anyone in the history of the game, records likely to stand forever.

In all matches that season, he scored 3816 runs with 18 centuries and a batting average of 90.85. For Middlesex, he scored 2467 runs and an average of 102.79. He never reached 200 in a county game, yet his average at Lord's was over 120 a match.

His first century that season came against Worcestershire, following an unbeaten 88 made in the first innings. After he'd hit 151 against Leicestershire, he turned in a sustained spell of bowling, using his 'chinamen' to take 5 for 108 as Middlesex won by 10 wickets. Northamptonshire also fell to Compton's all-round skills, as he took 6 for 78 after hitting 110, Middlesex winning by 8 wickets. However, his best all-round performance that season was against Surrey at the Oval where he scored 137 not out and took 6 for 94 and 6 for 80. His finest innings though, must surely have been his 168 against Kent at Lord's when Doug Wright was in full flight on a wicket that was in his favour.

When Middlesex played the Rest of England at the Oval in September of this year, he scored 246 to pass Tom Hayward's record aggregate (it was the second highest score he made for Middlesex). He was forced to retire with knee trouble shortly after reaching fifty, the legacy of that football injury; it was to cast a shadow on his career in later years.

As a bowler, he could spin the ball left handed from the back of the hand; what's more, he was really a very dangerous bowler of his kind whenever he found the correct length. He had been used sparingly as a bowler before the war, but in 1947, he took 73 wickets (his previous highest had been 22).

The summer of 1948 was a wet one, though he and Edrich added 424 for the third wicket in the match against Somerset – it remains the highest third wicket stand ever made in county cricket and his score of 252 not out (3 sixes and 37 fours) was his highest score for Middlesex.

In the Trent Bridge Test of 1948, England batted a second time, 344 behind. Washbrook and Edrich soon went, before Hutton and Compton took the score to 150 before Sir Leonard was bowled. In dreadful light, Compton defended against Keith Miller at his fiercest, hitting 184 in ten minutes short of 7 hours, before he instinctively hooked at a short delivery, slipped on the greasy turf and fell on his wicket.

At Old Trafford in the same series, he composed what is often cited as his greatest innings. At 33 for 2, he hooked a Lindwall no-ball on to his forehead and after stitches, returned with the England score on 119 for 5. Of England's total of 363, he scored 145 not out in five hours 27 minutes.

He scored 562 runs in the Tests (average 62.44) the most runs for a series in England against Australia. In 1948-49 he scored 300 not out in 181 minutes for the MCC v North-Eastern Transvaal at Benoni – it is still the fastest triple hundred in all first-class cricket. He celebrated his benefit game v Sussex the following summer with an outstanding innings. He treated the large Whit Monday crowd to an exhilarating piece of batsmanship; he took two and three quarter hours to reach 103, but then hit 79 in a minute short of three-quarters of an hour. His benefit raised £12,600 (easily a Middlesex record at the time) but was less than had been expected or what he deserved!

Denis Compton had genius – he was a national folk-hero of his time and his face looked down at you from billboards all over the country in an advertisement for hair cream. One day at Old Trafford, he was fielding in the slips when a strong wind forced him to keep sweeping the hair out of his eyes, causing a wit in the crowd to shout 'Why don't yer use Brylcreem Compton?' At which he nearly fell over himself with laughter.

As vice-captain of the 1950-51 team to Australia and New Zealand, he became the first professional to lead an MCC team in the field; seven years later, he turned amateur.

Along with Edrich, he was appointed joint-captain of Middlesex. He was still an automatic choice for the Test side and this coupled with his knee problem, which required a lot of rest, meant his appearances for Middlesex were limited. Even so, he hit three hundreds in the championship in May.

In the season of 1952, he was judged a failure yet, in all cricket, he scored 1880 runs (Average 39.16) and took 77 wickets at 28.58! At the end of the summer, he tendered his resignation as captain, feeling that it was better for the county if one man did the job, namely Edrich, Denis becoming vice-captain.

He still batted with a great sense of adventure, despite having undergone three knee operations, suffered periodic inflammation and been greatly troubled by lumbago. On his 35th birthday he hit an unbeaten 143 against Sussex (Syd Brown's benefit match).

However, during 1955 and 1956 he was forced to miss many matches as his knee trouble hampered him. His only hundred in 1955 was on Whit Monday as he took 150 off the hapless Sussex attack. In 1956, he almost scored another Test century against Australia, failing by six runs, after he'd been recalled to England's colours following an operation to remove a knee cap – it was his last Test appearance.

He played in 78 Tests, scoring 5807 runs at of 50.06. His top score of 278 came against Pakistan at Trent Bridge in 1954.

I'm sure he won't mind me commenting, but his reputation as one of the (if not the) most dreadful run-callers has survived to this day. R M V Robins' famous saying was that 'Compton calls for a run, remember it's only a basis for discussion' Perhaps the unofficial world record is held by Denis, who whilst making a century in brother Leslie's benefit match, managed to run out five men in the one innings, including the beneficiary himself!

Of course, Denis has never been famed for his punctuality and sense of responsibility and from time to time they have led to a minor disagreement with the authorities, but even then he only received the mildest of rebukes.

His last game as a professional came in the final championship match of the 1957 season at Lord's against Worcestershire, He scored 143 (a six and 17 fours) and 48 – it couldn't have ended any other way.

In all matches, he scored 38,942 first-class runs with 123 centuries. On his beloved Lord's he scored 16,732 runs at an average of 48.08 and with 48 centuries.

The golden boy of Middlesex and England cricket, he is one of the most remembered and popular players of all-time.

NORMAN COWANS

Born: 17 April 1961, Enfield, Jamaica
Played: 1980–

FIRST-CLASS MIDDLESEX RECORDS

Matches	*Innings*	*NO*	*Runs*	*HS*	*Ave*	*100s*
170	180	47	1227	66	9.23	0

Runs	*Wkts*	*Ave*	*Best*	*5wI*	*Ct*
11480	503	22.82	6–31	19	38

TEST MATCHES: 19

Born in Enfield St Mary, Jamaica in April 1961, Norman George Cowans arrived in England at the age of 11 from a background dominated by cricket.

He attended Park High School in Stanmore, but it was a non-cricket playing school. With the help of his Maths teacher, Paul Lucas, he started a cricket team which reached the final of the Harrow Schools competition in its first year of entry. Cowans was both captain and opening bowler and his progress was such that his teacher suggested he joined a club.

It was in 1973, that he joined the North London Polytechnic team to play colts cricket.

At 15, he was a regular first-team player for the colts and Paul Lucas recommended Norman to Middlesex Schools, for whom he played in 1976. In 1977 at the age of 16, he began to emerge as a future England prospect, when he fought his way through to the final five of the 'Find a Fast Bowler for England' competition. He went for trials in an attempt to get onto the Middlesex staff. It was two years later when he was accepted and joined the MCC staff.

While he was on the MCC staff, he played well for the County 2nd XI and was chosen for the Young England squad on their six week tour of Australia. His best performance was 4 for 49 off 14 overs in the second of the two Tests. However, his progress was halted in 1979 by a back injury caused by putting too much into his bowling at the MCC indoor school; it put him out for the summer.

The following season, was one of rebuilding for Cowans, but his success in the 2nd XI meant that when key players in the 1st team were playing Test cricket, he was given the opportunity in a couple of matches.

At the end of the season, he won a place on the Middlesex tour of Zimbabwe. In 1981, he was contracted to Middlesex and played in 12 Second XI Championship matches, taking 54 wickets at 15.77 runs apiece – a record in the Middlesex 2nd XI Championship. In his debut match the previous season against Lancashire, he took 4 for 26 off 12 overs to win the Man of the Match Award. His Championship debut was against Leicestershire when he took 5 for 58. He was also chosen for *The Cricketer* tour to Dubai where he was received with great enthusiasm; later spending the remainder of the winter with Claremont Cottesloe CC in Perth, Australia.

After pulling ligaments in his back early in 1982, he had to prove his fitness in the 2nd XI. It wasn't long though before he forced his way back into the 1st XI and a permanent place. He took 5 for 28 against Somerset and 5 for 34 v Gloucestershire and so with just 43 wickets behind him from his 16 first-class matches, he was selected to tour Australia with England, making his Test debut on that trip.

He was the first black Jamaican to represent England in an official Test and the 500th player. At Perth, he hit 36 and at Melbourne, bowled magnificently to take 6 for 77. He has played in 19 Tests and taken 51 wickets at 39.27 runs each.

When Middlesex beat Essex by 4 runs in the Benson and Hedges Cup Final, Cowans was the top wicket-taker in the match with 4 for 39 from his 10.1 overs. Early in the innings, he had taken quite a mauling from Gooch and Hardie but returned to have both Turner and David East caught and then york Foster. He had taken these wickets in four balls; the game finishing at 8.50 pm.

He toured Pakistan and New Zealand in the 1983-84 close season and at Lahore took 5 wickets in 22 balls, including three in his eleventh over.

He continued his progress as one of the most attacking opening bowlers in the country. The 1984 season was his best at the time, as he took 71 wickets at 19.52 runs each. The following summer, he took 6 for 31 against Leicestershire in mid-August as Middlesex won by ten wickets – these remain his best figures in first-class cricket.

He continued to bowl well in one-day finals and in the Benson and Hedges Final of 1986 when Middlesex beat Kent by 2 runs, he took 2 for 18 off 9 overs to rock the hop county at the beginning of their innings.

In 1987, he missed many matches through having to undergo a hernia operation, though he ended the season at the top of the Middlesex bowling averages with 44 wickets at 17.75 runs each.

His most successful season to date came in 1988 when he took 71 wickets at 18.16 runs each, including match figures of 10 for 97 against Warwickshire at Uxbridge.

A quiet and likeable cricketer, he played 13 Tests for England before being awarded his county cap by Middlesex.

WAYNE DANIEL

Born: 16 January 1956, St Philip, Barbados
Played: 1977–1988

FIRST-CLASS MIDDLESEX RECORDS

Matches	*Innings*	*NO*	*Runs*	*HS*	*Ave*	*100s*
213	187	86	1043	53*	10.32	0

Runs	*Wkts*	*Ave*	*Best*	*5wI*	*Ct*
15089	685	22.02	9–61	22	52

TEST MATCHES: 10 (West Indies)

Wayne Daniel was destined for greatness from his schooldays when he was a legendarily quick bowler even by Barbadian standards.

He was first approached by Middlesex in 1974 after touring with the West Indies Young Cricketers. The next year, he played some qualifying games and the county offered him terms for 1976. That spring however, he was selected as a raw 19 year old for the full West Indies squad to tour England. He was alongside illustrious names like Holding, Roberts and Holder; on the tour, he picked up 52 wickets. He had played in five Tests and was on the verge of an outstanding career in Test cricket.

In 1976-77 when Daniel was injured, Croft and Garner emerged to join Holding and Roberts. Then along came the World Series Cricket in which he was involved, allowing players like Sylvester Clarke and Malcolm Marshall to get their chance. After that, Daniel was always one of many with the likes of Eldine Baptiste and Winston Davis. It was some seven years later that he added another five appearances to his name.

In 1977, his first season for MIddlesex, he played a great part in the county's success. He finished third in the national bowling averages with 71 wickets as the county shared the Championship with Kent.

In his early years, he was without doubt among the fastest in the world and in 1978 turned in two outstanding performances in the Benson and Hedges Cup – 7 for 12 v Minor Counties East at Ipswich and 6 for 17 v Sussex at Hove.

Middlesex signed Vincent van der Bijl for the 1980 season as a replacement for Daniel, who everyone expected would be in the West Indian touring party – he wasn't and so the county had the unexpected bonus of being able to bowl two great bowlers together.

Nicknamed 'The Diamond' by Mike Smith, he put in an enormous effort on slow pitches at Lord's and elsewhere, fit to break a fast bowlers heart. When he did get on a quicker pitch, such as Hove in that 1980 season, he was devastating and finished with 6 for 15 in the Gillette Cup encounter.

In 1981, he performed the only hat-trick of his first-class career against

Lancashire at Southport. He also helped Keith Tomlins add 122 runs for an undefeated tenth wicket stand against Yorkshire at Lord's, Daniel scoring 53 not out. The following season, he produced his best figures with the ball for Middlesex, taking 9 for 61 against Glamorgan at Swansea.

Throughout his career, his insatiable appetite for wickets has shone through. In the Sunday League, he proved himself very adaptable, taking many wickets off a 15-yard run and only allowing the batsmen around 3 runs an over in that competition.

He never really felt secure in Test cricket, always an outsider and usually bowled as first change. His best performance was his 5 for 39 against India at Ahmedabad in 1983-84. Why with all his achievements and versatility he wasn't used more for his country was a mystery. Perhaps the answer lies in the suggestion that there was no love lost between West Indies captain Clive Lloyd and Wayne. In the 1981 match at Southport, seeing Daniel bowl to Lloyd would most certainly have supported that point of view.

Wayne Daniel was a great bowler, but for Middlesex and not for his country. He would pound in from the pavilion end at Lord's and could usually be relied upon to snap up some early wickets. If a stand developed, he was the one brought back to break it.

The Middlesex Committee generously decided to bring forward his benefit year to 1985, realising that strike bowlers depreciate much quicker than other assets. In terms of the number of Championship wickets it was his most profitable summer, Daniel capturing 79 wickets at 26.72 runs each.

An amusing man within the dressing-room, he could still generate a lively pace towards the end of his career, though generally, he wasn't the force to be reckoned with that he had been.

Throughout the 1987 season he suffered increasingly from fast bowler's niggles and in 1988 he only played in two matches.

Wayne Daniel was a great success not only for his bowling but also as a part of Middlesex cricket with a genuine interest in seeing the county's young players develop. Totally committed to the cause of Middlesex cricket, it was easy to forget that he was an overseas player.

A gentle, sensitive soul, Wayne Wendell Daniel just drifted away from the first-class game.

PAUL DOWNTON

Born: 4 April 1957, Farnborough, Kent
Played: 1980–1991

FIRST-CLASS MIDDLESEX RECORDS

Matches	*Innings*	*NO*	*Runs*	*HS*	*Ave*	*100s*
205	283	53	6670	126*	28.87	6

Runs	*Wkts*	*Ave*	*Best*	*5wI*	*Ct*	*St*
9	1	9.00	1-4	0	436	58

TEST MATCHES: 30

Born a man of Kent, Paul Rupert Downton attended both Sevenoaks Prep and Sevenoaks School, where he played as an all-rounder when he first played for the Under-13 team. However, within twelve months, he was playing as wicket-keeper, a position in which he had always shown interest.

Paul received great help from Alan Hurd, a player with both Cambridge and Essex and his cricket master and English tutor. During his six seasons in the Sevenoaks School side, they were unbeaten for three of them. After moving up through the various Sevenoaks XIs he made his debut for the Kent 2nd XI at the age of 16.

He had a fairly uninterrupted journey leading him to sign for Kent in 1976. His father George, was well known in Kent cricketing circles and represented the county in the late forties when Godfrey Evans was on Test duty. His Kent 1st team debut came in 1977 as Kent entertained Surrey at Maidstone; his brilliant stumping of Alan Butcher off Asif Iqbal going a long way towards Paul winning a surprise tour place.

During his time with Kent, he scored 396 runs and helped dismiss 99 batsmen.

During the winter of 1979, the Kent committee offered Alan Knott a long term contract and so Paul Downton had no option but to look elsewhere. John Murray rated him very highly and so when Paul approached the county, the offer of a contract was made. He was told that he would have no guarantee of a place, but to many people's surprise, he still opted for Middlesex.

He was still completing his law studies at Exeter University during the first half of that 1980 season, and must have wondered if he'd made the right move as Ian Gould was playing very well.

After a few weeks in the 2nd XI, he was given an opportunity to open the batting with Mike Brearley against Kent at the end of July – this partnership going a long way to help the side win the Championship.

In that 1980 season, he hit an unbeaten 90 against Derbyshire at Uxbridge and 64 and 67 against Essex, finishing the season with 521 runs from nine matches and an average of 40.07. At the end of the season, he was chosen to tour the West Indies with the England side; some four years after he'd been vice-captain of the England Young Cricketers tour to the Caribbean.

Paul Downton was an all-rounder rather than a specialist, being a good middle-order batsman and a resolute wicket-keeper. Against Nottinghamshire at Lord's in 1981 he took 6 catches in an innings and made eight dismissals in the match. The county from Trent Bridge must rank among Downton's favourite opposition as he has hit his best scores in the Nat West (62 in 1984) and the John Player League (70 in 1985) on that ground.

He has represented England in 30 Tests, though he has occasionally lost his place as wicket-keeper due to missing a relatively easy chance, but regained it before long with his batting ability. His highest Test score is 74, made against India at Delhi in 1984-85. He has helped to dismiss 75 batsmen, and took 4 catches in Australia's second innings at the Oval in 1985.

Also in 1985, he hit his maiden first-class hundred, 104 (with 13 fours) as he and Clive Radley added 289 for the fifth wicket against Northamptonshire at Uxbridge; ending the season with 663 runs and an average of 44.20. The highest score of his first-class career, came in 1986 when he hit 126 against Oxford University.

His best season with the bat to date is 1987, when he hit 1120 first-class runs, 995 of them in the County Championship. Against Hampshire at Southampton that summer, he hit an unbeaten 80, his highest score in the Benson and Hedges competition.

In 1990, he suffered a freak eye injury, that led to his retirement after three matches in 1991. He was hit by a bail during the county's Sunday League match against Hampshire. The bail flew into Downton's eye after Hampshire batsman Julian Wood had been bowled by John Emburey. It was Paul Downton's benefit year and initially he was kept in Basingstoke General Hospital before being transferred to the St John and St Elizabeth Hospital in St John's Wood from where he was released after several days.

On the retirement of Yorkshire's David Bairstow, he became the leading wicket-keeper in terms of f irst-class dismissals (766) still in the game – a worthy member of Middlesex's continuing line of outstanding wicket-keepers.

JACK DURSTON

Born: 11 July 1893, Clophill, Bedfordshire
Died: 8 April 1965
Played: 1919–1933

FIRST-CLASS MIDDLESEX RECORDS

Matches	*Innings*	*NO*	*Runs*	*HS*	*Ave*	*100s*
349	434	127	3569	92*	11.63	0

Runs	*Wkts*	*Ave*	*Best*	*5wI*	*Ct*
25877	1178	21.97	8-27	65	230

TEST MATCHES: 1

Born at Clophill in Bedfordshire, Jack Durston learned his cricket with his local club before becoming a ground-staff boy at Lord's in 1914.

He could move the ball considerably and at great pace, but he was handicapped somewhat by the fact that he could never get his arm absolutely straight.

During the war, he served in the Royal Engineers. He returned for his first season in the Middlesex side in 1919, playing in five matches and taking just 5 wickets at a cost of 74.20 runs each. His interests didn't just centre around cricket, for at 6ft 5ins, he was a more than adequate goalkeeper for Brentford F.C.

Jack Durston made great strides after his initial season in the Middlesex side; so much so, that he was almost England class within twelve months of making his debut. During the next two seasons, he hardly had one bad match. Initially, he was quite a wild bowler, but he benefited greatly from coaching and advice and was able to add much more control to his blistering pace. He ended the 1920 season with 113 wickets, going a long way in helping Middlesex win the County Championship. He took nine wickets at Lord's as Hampshire were beaten by 9 wickets. In the return match with Hampshire at Southampton, he again took nine wickets and then nine again as Nottinghamshire were beaten by 9 wickets.

In 1921, he began to form a very successful opening bowling partnership with Nigel Haig and ended the season with 111 championship wickets, 136 in all matches at 19.50 runs each. He represented the Players against the Gentlemen at Lord's and in the match against Surrey, a match Middlesex only had to draw to win the championship for a second successive year, he had match figures of 7 for 103, including clean bowling Sandham in both innings.

Also in 1921, he turned in an outstanding performance against Warwick Armstrong's Australians with match figures of 11 for 149, including 7 for 84 in their first innings. It was this performance that led to his selection for England in the second Test against Australia at Lord's and though he took

5 wickets for 136 runs, he was never chosen again. He in fact took 4 for 102 in Australia's total of 342 and was probably the best of the English bowlers. He returned to Middlesex and continued to bowl consistently well.

He performed the hat-trick on two occasions; against Cambridge University in 1922, when he took 6 for 29 and then against Oxford University the following year when he had figures of 8 for 27.

In 1924, in the match Middlesex lost by 61 runs after bowling out Gloucestershire for 31, Durston took 4 for 18 in the West Country sides' disastrous innings.

His batting was of negligible value, though it did improve as his career progressed. In 1927, he and Patsy Hendren added 160 in eighty minutes against Essex to establish the Middlesex ninth wicket record partnership. However, his top score of 92 not out came against Northamptonshire in 1930 after he'd hit 51 in the first innings.

In 1927, for the first time in his career, he had to bowl over 1000 overs, this despite having to miss the last thirteen matches due to a strain.

The lengthy spells of bowling were getting beyond Durston and so in 1928 he began bowling slow-medium off-breaks and his days as a pure out and out fast bowler were over. However, he still had a good summer taking over 100 wickets. Though handicapped by knee trouble in the summer of 1929, he still took 75 wickets in all matches and in 1930, ended the season with 619 runs, a great improvement on past seasons with the bat!

By 1932, his weight had increased to almost 20 stone, but he had an Indian summer, picking up 102 wickets at 19.55 runs apiece. In Middlesex's opening match of the season against Warwickshire, he helped dismiss the first four batsmen for nought.

His playing career came to a close at the end of the 1933 season when he was appointed coach and captained the 2nd XI. He also ran an indoor coaching school, putting something back into the game.

He had toured Argentina twice, in 1929 with Julien Cahn's team and then again in 1937-38 with Sir Theodore Brinckman's side.

An honest player, taking wickets year after year throughout the twenties he died in hospital at Southall on 8 April 1965, aged 71.

PHIL EDMONDS

Born: 8 March 1951, Lusaka, N. Rhodesia
Played: 1971–1987

FIRST-CLASS MIDDLESEX RECORDS

Matches	*Innings*	*NO*	*Runs*	*HS*	*Ave*	*1OOs*
253	311	57	5037	142	19.83	2

Runs	*Wkts*	*Ave*	*Best*	*5wI*	*Ct*
20755	879	23.61	8-53	3	235

TEST MATCHES: 51

Phil Edmonds was born in Lusaka of a Belgian mother and a British father.

His family left Rhodesia when Phil was 15 and set up home in Kent, Phil attending Skinner's School in Tunbridge Wells and later Cranbrook, where he skippered the 1st XI. At the age of seventeen, he was relieved of the captaincy of the School side – rated too good and the rest of the side not up to his standard! At this time, he also played a few games for the Kent 2nd XI. He may have been too advanced for the School XI, but he enjoyed playing Club cricket for an Ashford village side in Kent.

He went up to Cambridge, where Majid Khan was the captain. It was under his leadership that he began to turn himself into a formidable cricketer.

In only his second game for the University against Leicestershire, he took nine wickets. There were many counties after his signature, but Phil chose Middlesex and made his debut for them in 1971 against Essex, taking five wickets. In that first summer, he played in five matches and collected 14 wickets.

He left Cambridge in 1973 after captaining the side and taking 78 wickets in his three years at a cost of 29.54, to concentrate on playing full-time for Middlesex. His best figures in his time at Cambridge, were 7 for 56 against Oxford University at Lord's in 1971.

In his first full season, 1974, he took 73 wickets for Middlesex, including 7 for 8 against Kent at Canterbury and 6 for 22 against Surrey at Lord's. He won his county cap and then in the winter, he was elected Young Cricketer of the Year by the Cricket Writers Club.

In 1975, he was selected for England for the first time against Australia at Headingley, In his first 12 overs, he took five wickets for 17 runs. His victims were Ian Chappell and Ross Edwards (with successive deliveries), Greg Chappell, Doug Walters and Max Walker. His final analysis was:

O	*M*	*R*	*W*
20	7	28	5

Sadly, the match itself, delicately poised, was ruined by the acts of a few lunatics who vandalised the pitch on the fourth evening. He ended the

1975 season with 65 wickets for Middlesex, including 7 for 48 against Hampshire at Southampton.

In 1976, he hit his maiden first-class century, 103 not out when playing for T N Pearce's XI against the West Indians at Scarborough; in fact, it was a good match for Edmonds, as he took 6 for 67. There was a great deal of interest in his batting position, for at one stage, it looked as though he might emulate even the great Wilfred Rhodes by batting at number 1.

The following season, he took 80 wickets for Middlesex at 23.04, his best performance being 8 for 132 against Gloucestershire in their second innings at Lord's (14 for 150 in the match) and 6 for 27 against Lancashire at Blackpool, in a game I remember well.

He toured Pakistan and New Zealand in 1977-78, producing the best return of his Test career, 7 for 66 at Karachi – it unquestionably saved the entire series for England. At the time, it was the best ever for a Test innings in Pakistan and remains the best for England in that country. It was a record-breaking effort and it ensured the draw. He also hit his first half-century at Test level, scoring exactly 50 in the second Test against New Zealand at Christchurch.

The following summer, he had a most successful time with the ball in the return series against Pakistan and New Zealand. His analysis of:

0	*M*	*R*	*W*
8	6	6	4

against Pakistan at Lord's is one of the best in Test history. He took 8 wickets against Pakistan at 11.88 runs apiece and 10 against New Zealand at a cost of 14.50 runs each. For Middlesex, he continued to turn in some remarkable performances; 7 for 4 against Leicestershire and 6 for 36 against Nottinghamshire, both at Lord's.

He had a disappointing time with the ball over the next two seasons, but his first century for Middlesex, 142 against Glamorgan at Swansea came in 1979. He also played a quite extraordinary innings at Worcester in 1982, making 92 with a completely untreated piece of willow from a local factory – it was totally devoid of logo, shape or rubber grip! He was a beautifully clean hitter of the ball but was strangely inconsistent with the bat.

In 1981, he was back to something like his old self, taking 73 wickets for Middlesex at 24.85. His best performance was 6 for 93 against Derbyshire, though he did take a hat-trick against Leicestershire at Grace Road.

He took a similar number of wickets for Middlesex the following season at a better average, 20.21, as well as playing in three Tests against India. He took 8 for 80 against Sussex, 6 for 31 against Nottinghamshire (both at Lord's) and 6 for 48 against Hampshire at Uxbridge.

In 1983, he had his best season for Middlesex, taking 88 wickets at 19.92 runs each. In June of this year, he took 54 first-class wickets at an average of 12.33 – he hadn't taken a first-class wicket previously that season! He had four hauls of six wickets in an innings: 6 for 38(v Derbyshire) 6 for 49 (v Cambridge University) 6 for 87 (v Surrey) and 6 for 93 (v New Zealand).

He was no-balled when playing for England against New Zealand at the Oval in 1983, for bowling two bouncers in an over – certainly a rare instance by a slow bowler (but not perhaps if your name is Phil Edmonds).

He played in 51 Test matches, scoring 975 runs at an average of 17.50 with a top score of 64 against India at Lord's in 1982. With the ball, he took 125 wickets at 34.18, with that superb performance in Karachi his best.

In 1984, he produced his best figures with the ball, 8 for 53 against Hampshire at Bournemouth – surely his most popular county when one looks at his performances against them over the years. On 21st August this season, he took his 1000th first-class wicket in dismissing Tim Boon of Leicestershire when Middlesex played at Grace Road.

He was one of the new brigade of cricketers brandishing briefcases instead of holdalls – he was no ordinary cricketer and certainly no ordinary man. He was a man about whom gossip tended to gather, but as a cricketer, he was greatly respected amongst his fellow professionals.

He had never really been satisfied with the lot of the cricketer. His business empire had grown so much, that he didn't have the time needed to devote to the professional game. His proposal to Middlesex was that he should play as an amateur, practising on free evenings and picking his own games – not surprisingly, the Middlesex Committee threw out the idea.

He had stayed with Middlesex for over 15 years and had served them well. He was a dedicated and motivated professional, playing with fun, yet he played hard to win.

A richly gifted cricketer, he was among the most talented of players.

BILL EDRICH

Born: 26 March 1916, Lingwood, Norfolk
Died: 23 April 1986
Played: 1937–1958

FIRST-CLASS MIDDLESEX RECORDS

Matches	*Innings*	*NO*	*Runs*	*HS*	*Ave*	*100s*
389	658	65	25738	267*	43.40	62

Runs	*Wkts*	*Ave*	*Best*	*5wI*	*Ct*	*St*
9975	328	30.41	7-48	10	382	1

TEST MATCHES: 39

Born into a cricketing family, one of the best treats he and his brothers enjoyed was the annual August Bank Holiday visit to Lakenham to see Norfolk play Hertfordshire. They had seen their father and uncle play village cricket, but this was something special, At the age 10, Bill along with brother Eric, who was two years his senior, went to Bracondale. It was here that Bill received expert coaching from the old Worcestershire and Staffordshire all-rounder Jack Nichols.

In 1929 at the age of 13, he got his school colours and one year later, took all ten Norwich High School wickets (all clean bowled!) for 18 runs in 49 balls. Despite his tender age, he was made captain and later in that year of 1930, hit his first century, 121 against Diss Secondary School.

At the age of 16, after some very impressive performances, he was given his first game for the Norfolk County side against All India at Lakenham. Norfolk were dismissed for 49, only Bill Edrich with 20 reaching double figures. Wisden commenting: 'Edrich a schoolboy batted in promising fashion.'

In April 1934, he went to Lord's for a trial and joined the MCC second-class ground-staff, yet was available to play for Norfolk during the qualification period. He represented the MCC that summer, scoring 55 at Oxford and 6 on his first appearance at Lord's against Cambridge University. At the end of that season, he had a trial with Tottenham Hotspur and was given a contract to join the nursery at Northfleet.

In 1935, he scored a superb 111 out of Norfolk's 194 in the match against the South African tourists. At the end of that season, he was called into the office of the MCC Secretary at Lord's to be told that he wouldn't be qualified for Middlesex the next season as the forms from Norfolk failed to arrive until October 1934 and it was a full two year qualification period. During the winter months, he played a game in the Spurs first team against Blackpool at White Hart Lane.

The following season, his opportunities in first-class cricket were limited to nine innings, but he hit three centuries; his first 114 in the match against Surrey, his others against Oxford University and Kent.

In 1937, he made his first century for Middlesex in the match against Lancashire at Lord's. Middlesex's score was 2 for 2, but Edrich batted for four hours 20 minutes to score 175 out of his sides reply of 369 to Lancashire's first innings total of 233. Lancashire made 309 in their second innings to set Middlesex 174 to win. The wicket was now affected by rain, but Bill batted magnificently to make 73 not out, though Lancashire won by 22 runs. Wisden regarded the innings as the best played by anyone that season. He ended his first full season with 2154 runs at an average of 44.87 with three hundreds.

During the winter of 1937-38, he had to bid farewell to his football career with Spurs as he accepted the offer to tour India with a team under the sponsorship and captaincy of Lord Tennyson. He adapted himself to the conditions, topping the batting averages for both the five unofficial Tests and for all matches. On his debut in India, he carried his bat for 140 out of 303 against Sind at Karachi.

The 1938 season began with Bill hitting 104 against Yorkshire and 115 against Surrey, playing for the MCC in both matches. In only his second game for Middlesex, he took 182 and 71 off a Gloucestershire attack that included Tom Goddard and Reg Sinfield. Against Nottinghamshire at Lord's he hit Larwood and Voce to all parts of the ground in scoring a magnificent 245. Due to the generosity of Don Bradman, Bill was able to reach 1000 runs before the end of May; in Middlesex's match against the Australians, only twenty minutes remained when The Don declared, setting Middlesex 59 to win – a noble gesture by the great Australian. Bill was the fifth Englishman after W G Grace Hayward, Hammond and Hallows to achieve this feat. All his runs were scored at Lord's and it remains the only pre-June 1000 to include a duck! He continued to score heavily in county cricket for Middlesex, but in six Test match innings that summer, he only scored 67 runs, yet was named in the touring party for South Africa.

He failed with the bat in the first four Tests, but made a sparkling 219 in England's second innings of the fifth and final Test after South Africa had set the tourists 696 to win!

In 1939, he scored 2186 runs at an average of 51.28 with seven centuries, but wasn't included in any of the Tests against the West Indies. He had scored over 2000 runs in each of his first three seasons in the Middlesex side and was one of the 'Five Cricketers of the Year' in the 1940 edition of Wisden. No batsman had ever had three such opening years, but of course Edrich, though only 21 in 1937 was an experienced player.

He was a complete batsman with a magnificent defence and a wide range of attacking strokes. He was a superb and absolutely fearless hooker of the fastest bowling but also very quick on his feet against the spinners and his cutting was of the highest order. Even on the larger grounds, he was able to play a lofted stroke wide of mid-on, which was a cross between the on-drive and the 'cow-shot', this brought him a vast number of sixes.

At the outbreak of war, Bill volunteered for flying duties with the RAF. He was promoted to flight commander and won the DFC. In 1945, he played in all of the Victory Test Matches against Australia, topping the batting averages with 47.28.

In 1946, he began the summer badly, but came good in the second half of the season, scoring a superb 127 not out from a total of 169 against Gloucestershire. The knock was all the more remarkable, as the only Middlesex batsman to score more than 6 was Price with 2. Bill put more into his cricket that summer, over a short space of time than anyone else, his top score being 222 not out v Northamptonshire. He realised that if he was to win back his England place, he must produce some good bowling and fielding. The results of his hard work were beginning to show; 5 for 30 v Kent; 4 for 71 v Sussex; 7 for 48 v Worcestershire and then 7 for 69 v Northamptonshire, including the first six in the order.

He was selected to tour Australia in 1946-47 and against Queensland in the final match before the first Test, he was the only English batsman to master the leg-spin of Colin McCool, scoring 64 not out and 71. In that first Test, he batted skilfully for 13 hours in making 16 on a wicket affected by an overnight thunderstorm as Lindwall struck him repeatedly. England lost the second Test at Sydney, but Edrich made his mark with 71 and 119 (his first century against Australia). In the third Test, he made a brave 89 after being struck a terrible blow to the inside of the knee whilst fielding in Australia's first innings. He ended the series with England's highest aggregate of 462 runs at an average of 46.20.

In 1947, Bill had the offer of a commercial career if he turned amateur. In his first game against Somerset, he scored 102 and then took 4 for 5 the next morning, but the West Country side won a marvellous match by one wicket. He hadn't the build of a fast bowler, but his aggression and endeavour made him as quick as anyone in that 1947 season. In the next match, he had match figures of 8 for 54 and then followed it with 225 against Warwickshire. Bill reached his 1000 runs on June 20th, in three innings less than Denis Compton and though it was ten days after Denis had reached the landmark, he overtook him in the race to 2000. In the absence of both Robins and Mann, he was given the opportunity to captain Middlesex for the first time against Leicestershire at Grace Road. He made what seemed a bad decision in asking Leicestershire to bat first when they made 309. Middlesex's reply was to score 637 for 4 with Edrich making 257 not out(4 sixes and 24 fours) and Compton 151. Leicestershire replied with 393, leaving Middlesex just 25 minutes to get the 66 runs needed. The runs were made in just seven overs with four minutes remaining. He hit the highest score of his career at Northampton, 267 not out; it was made in 5 hours and contained three sixes and 24 fours.

In the Test series against South Africa, he headed both the batting and bowling averages with 552 runs (Average 110.40) and 16 wickets (Average 23.12). His top score being 191 made in the third Test at Old Trafford.

Towards the end of the 1947 season, he scored 157 not out against Surrey on a day when Middlesex scored 537 for 2; all this with a torn muscle under the right shoulder. He went on in the final game, Champion County v The Rest, to score 180 to pass Tom Hayward's record aggregate of 3518 runs, already surpassed by Denis Compton.

In 1948, he scored 2428 runs, including six centuries at an average of 49.55. Against Somerset at Lord's, he and Denis Compton set a new Middlesex record for the third wicket, when they added an unbeaten 424. The following season, he scored 2253 runs at an average of 39.52 with a top score of 182. He played in all four Tests against New Zealand, averaging 54.00 from his aggregate of 324 runs.

In making 134 against Northamptonshire he 'hit' a nine! There were no restricted boundaries in those days and Bill hit a lofted on-drive towards the Nursery clock. Dennis Brookes chased after it and Freddie Brown intercepted the throw, only to then throw the ball at the wicket at the pavilion end and see the ball deflected to the pavilion rails for four more to add to the five that Bill and Syd Brown had already run!

After playing in the first two Tests of 1950 against the West Indies, he was dropped because he committed the indiscretion of arriving back in his hotel room sometime after midnight. In fact, he had to serve what amounted to a three-year suspension! In those days, a small indiscretion like Bill's could ruin a players career.

In 1951, though he only scored one century, he amassed 1773 runs. Wisden commented 'If the situation demanded caution or called for rapid progress, Edrich filled both roles with great distinction.' This was the first year that Bill Edrich shared the captaincy with Denis Compton, an arrangement that continued in 1952. That season, Bill scored 2101 runs (Average 41.19) with his top score 239 against Oxford University.

In 1953, the Middlesex Committee decided to appoint Bill as sole captain. England were involved in a tense and exciting series against Australia, but their batting was so fragile, that there was a country-wide demand for Bill Edrich. He was recalled for the third Test at Old Trafford, playing his part in the last three Tests as England regained the Ashes. In all matches that summer, he scored 2557 runs and averaged 47.35 – his top score being 211 v Essex at Lords (his second century of the season off the Essex attack).

The following season he scored 1783 runs at 39.62 with a top score of 195. In the match against Northamptonshire, he top-edged 'Typhoon' Tyson on to his cheek-bone and had to spend the night in hospital. He amazed everyone by appearing at the fall of the first wicket the following morning, the first ball from Tyson striking him over the heart. He struggled to find his form in 1955, though he did score 1642 runs in all matches at 28.31.

A good rest over the winter seemed to do the trick, Edrich returning for the 1956 season in a rejuvenated mood. He scored 1831 runs at 33.29 with a top score of 208 not out at Chesterfield in the match with Derbyshire (he was one of only eight batsmen in the country to hit a double century that season). His best performance however, was probably his 82 against Surrey on a spinner's paradise at the Oval – easily the top score in the match, thwarting both Laker and Lock.

At the end of the 1957 season, he decided to give up the Middlesex captaincy. As a captain whenever there was a slight chance of victory, he would always go for it, his methods often lifting Middlesex to a higher place in the County Championship than perhaps their merit deserved.

He played one more season for Middlesex, his one century coming in his last first-class match for the MCC against Cambridge University. When he received an offer to captain Norfolk in the Minor Counties competition in 1959, he was thrilled to accept. In 1970, he came back to Lord's with Norfolk for a Gillette Cup match and was his sides most successful batsman – at the age of 54, he hit 36 off 37 balls! He played for Norfolk until 1971; during those twelve years, he scored 8,034 runs (Average 35.08) with 9 centuries and took 415 wickets at 19.17, his best figures being 7 for 45 against Suffolk.

In August 1977, Norfolk's 150th Anniversary was celebrated by a match with MCC, who included Bill in their side.

In a first-class career spanning twenty-four years, he scored 36,965 runs with 86 hundreds and a career average of 42.19. He also took 479 wickets and claimed 522 catches.

Married five times, he was certainly a man who lived life to the full, playing his cricket the same way.

JOHN EMBUREY

Born: 20 August 1952, Peckham
Played: 1973–

FIRST-CLASS MIDDLESEX RECORDS

Matches	*Innings*	*NO*	*Runs*	*HS*	*Ave*	*100s*
292	372	73	7184	133	24.03	4

Runs	*Wkts*	*Ave*	*Best*	*5wI*	*Ct*
23269	953	24.42	7-27	46	291

TEST MATCHES: 60

Like most young boys, John Emburey just wanted to bowl as fast as he could, and this in the back streets of Peckham, where he was born and grew up, is what he did. It was good enough to get him into the South London Schools Under 10 and under 11 sides.

He attended Peckham Manor Secondary School, where at the age of 12, he accidentally discovered the art of off-spin bowling and was in the 1st XI three years early. When he was 16, he toured East Africa with the London Schools, later going on to play for both England Schools and Surrey Young Cricketers, with whom he toured Canada.

In the winter months after his tour to Canada, he attended the Surrey nets at Crystal Palace and was desperately keen to join his native county. However, a letter from Arthur McIntyre the Surrey coach brought great disappointment, for Surrey had three spinners on the staff already, one of which was Pat Pocock. McIntyre suggested to John, then a wages clerk with the Amalgamated Union of Engineering Workers, that he try Middlesex, but he was so dejected that he didn't even bother. Fortunately for John and Middlesex, Arthur McIntyre wrote on his behalf and Don Bennett invited him for a trial at Lord's in mid-season 1971. He impressed sufficiently to be given a three month contract for the second half of the season and has been on the staff ever since.

A few games in the 2nd XI followed before he made his first team debut in 1973. In 1974, he took 58 wickets in the 2nd XI and was beginning to get frustrated by the presence of Fred Titmus. In six seasons, he played no more than a dozen first-class matches for Middlesex. I suppose few on the county circuit had too high an opinion of Emburey when he played in those occasional games before he played on a regular basis in 1977. It was skipper Brearley who had faith in him and of course was proved right.

In fact, his six year apprenticeship went a long way in helping his first season to be a great success. In only 17 first-class matches, Emburey took 81 wickets and was rewarded with his county cap.

At the end of the season, he went to Australia as part of the Whitbread Scholarship, though there had been rather premature predictions made that he could be picked for England's winter tour of Pakistan and New Zealand.

Though overlooked for that tour, Test recognition was only a matter of waiting. It came with the announcement on his 26th birthday that he would play for England in the final Cornhill Test of the 1978 summer against New Zealand at Lord's. He made a remarkable start, dismissing Bruce Edgar with his fourth ball in Test cricket.

By 1980, Emburey had emerged as one of the world's leading off-spinners. In May of that season, he took 9 wickets as Middlesex beat Surrey by an innings to go top of the table. Towards the end of the season when Middlesex entertained Nottinghamshire, 19 wickets fell in a day 12 of them to John Emburey – Middlesex winning on the third morning.

John Emburey had a respect for Brearley and his ideas, but he always retained his own interpretation and solution to events.

Embers is an economical bowler compared with many of his ilk. He is a tall man, with a high easy action, able to combine accuracy with bounce, flight and subtle variations in pace,

He has been England's number one off-spin bowler over this last decade, even though he was banished from Test cricket from 1982–85, thus missing a possible 32 Tests. He is now serving yet another ban for his part in the visit to South Africa in 1989-90, or he could have played in well over 100 Tests.

He has played in 60 Tests, scoring 1540 runs at an average of 21.69 and a top score of 75 against New Zealand at Trent Bridge in 1986. At Colombo in the inaugural Test against Sri Lanka, he took 6 for 33 (including a spell of 5 for 5). In 1985, he took 5 for 82 against Australia at Headingley and on the 1985-86 tour of the Caribbean, he took 5 for 78 at Port of Spain, he was in superb form in England's success 'Down under' in 1986-87, taking 5 for 80 at Brisbane and then producing his best ever Test figures, 7 for 78 at Sydney. He has 138 Test wickets at an average of 36.99.

He won the Swanton Trophy in 1983 for being the first bowler to reach 100 wickets, and at the end of the season was chosen as one of Wisden's Five Cricketers of the Year.

He ended the season with 103 wickets at 17.88. Against Kent at Dartford, he took six of the first seven wickets to fall for only 13 runs and was very disappointed not to get at least two of the last three wickets as well – it was the best bowling of his career up to that time. Also by this season, his batting had improved so much, that he was a recognised number six. He helped Mike Gatting add 268 for the fifth wicket against Essex at Chelmsford, hitting his best ever score of 133. He also helped establish a Middlesex record for the fifth wicket in the John Player League as he and Roland Butcher added 109 against Gloucestershire at Lord's.

In 1983-84, he hit 6 sixes off 7 balls for Western Province against Eastern Province at Cape Town. In 1986-87, he established a world record by scoring 46 entirely in boundaries (a six and 10 fours) for an England Xl against Tasmania at Hobart.

John Emburey remains one of the few spinners to regularly bowl his quota of overs in all the limited-overs competitions, especially the one-day finals. His record:

	O	M	R	W
1983 Benson & Hedges v Essex	11	3	17	0
1984 Nat West v Kent	12	1	27	1
1986 Benson Hedges v Kent	11	5	16	0

In his autobiography 'Emburey' he suggested that he had virtually given up hope of the England captaincy, though he had been Middlesex's vice-captain since 1983, yet in 1988, he led his country twice in the disastrous home series against the West Indies.

In 1989, he produced the best bowling figures of his career, 7 for 27 (12 for 66 in the match) against Gloucestershire at Cheltenham.

In 1990 he hit a superb unbeaten 111 off 127 balls against Hampshire, his second fifty coming off 31 balls – his innings contained 4 sixes and 12 fours.

The exceptional features of Emburey's bowling have been the straightness of his line, from wicket to wicket and the accuracy of his length, which I'm sure will be seen around the county grounds for many seasons to come.

BOB GALE

Born: 10 December 1933, Old Warden, Bedfordshire
Played: 1956–1965

FIRST-CLASS MIDDLESEX RECORDS

Matches	*Innings*	*NO*	*Runs*	*HS*	*Ave*	*100s*
219	398	12	11234	200	29.10	13

Runs	*Wkts*	*Ave*	*Best*	*5wI*	*Ct*
1525	46	33.15	4-57	0	108

TEST MATCHES: 0

Bob Gale played his early cricket for the Army while on national service and so his Middlesex career didn't start until 1956.

Probably the most gifted of the young Middlesex players of that time, Bob Gale was a big man with great power in his strokes. There were occasions when he took the opposition attacks apart and certainly looked good enough to go on and represent his country.

However, there were times when Bob Gale looked quite ordinary, for between his big innings, there were barren patches. There were times even in the same innings that he looked quite ordinary. It is probably true to say that Bob Gale didn't actually know how good he could be. On receiving two balls which appeared similar in all respects, he would despatch the first majestically past the sight screen and play the other gently back to a much relieved bowler!

In 1958, Gale was the only Middlesex batsman to score a century in the county championship and he made two. It was during this season that he began his association with a new opening partner in Eric Russell. They opened the Middlesex innings for the first time in the match against Leicestershire with stands of 96 and 113; Gale's scores being 52 and 73.

In 1962, Gale passed 2000 runs for the season, including the highest score of his first-class career, 200 against Glamorgan at Newport.

Though he continued to play for Middlesex until 1965, after the summer of 1962, he was more businessman than cricketer. He retired at the age of just 31 with almost 12,000 first-class runs and 13 centuries to his name.

Elected to the General Committee in 1989, towards the end of the year, he took over from Mike Sturt as Chairman of the Cricket Sub-Committee.

MIKE GATTING

Born: 6 June 1957, Kingsbury
Played: 1975–

FIRST-CLASS MIDDLESEX RECORDS

Matches	*Innings*	*NO*	*Runs*	*HS*	*Ave*	*100s*
276	438	74	19291	258	53.00	52

Runs	*Wkts*	*Ave*	*Best*	*5wI*	*Ct*
3349	125	26.79	5-34	2	261

TEST MATCHES: 68

Mike Gatting was educated at the John Kelly Boys' High School, Cricklewood, though he played much of his early cricket with Brondesbury.

He was also a very good footballer and played for both Brent and Middlesex Schools. He was recommended to West Ham United as a fifth former, but nothing came of it. He had a trial with Queen's Park Rangers and was then offered an apprenticeship with Watford, but in his own mind, he knew he would become a professional cricketer.

He played cricket for Middlesex Under-15's for two seasons and hit a century for England Schools in their match against the Public Schools. In 1974, he represented England Young Cricketers and became a scholarship boy with The Cricket Society. He later went on a Whitbread Scholarship to Australia – there were no other distractions for Mike Gatting, except possibly for one – he won a bronze medal along with brother Steve (a professional footballer) at Neasden Ritz for ballroom dancing!

Although making his debut in 1975, it was the following season when he came to the fore. Against Sussex at Lord's, he took three wickets as the south coast side were bowled out for 90 and then hit 94 as Middlesex went on to win by an innings. During the close season, he toured the West Indies with the England Young Cricketers.

Middlesex captain Mike Brearley had great confidence in Gatting's ability – in his first full season, 1977, he hit 1095 runs, was awarded his county cap and at the end of the season was selected for England's winter tour of Pakistan and New Zealand, playing in two Tests.

In 1978, he hit his first century for Middlesex, 128 v Derbyshire and ended the season at the top of the Middlesex bowling averages with 24 wickets at 14.58 and a best of 5 for 59 v Leicestershire.

He was a surprise and I suppose controversial selection for the England World Cup Squad in 1979, yet he didn't play in a match. The following season he hit his highest score at that time, 136 v Surrey at Lord's and hit his first Test half-century, 56 v West Indies at Old Trafford.

In 1981, he increased his highest first-class score with a brilliant innings of 186 not out against Derbyshire. He ended the season with 1026 runs at an average of 68.40 – it was the first of four successive seasons that he was to top the Middlesex batting averages. At the end of the season, he was elected the Best Young Cricketer of the Year.

He seemed to be getting better with each season and in 1982, he played a superb innings of 192 v Surrey, yet Middlesex's efforts for victory were thwarted by the weather.

He was appointed captain of Middlesex in 1983, almost by default – Brearley was a hard act to follow, but Gatting rose to the challenge; he was different in every way to Brearley. There were certain things in his favour when he took over – he inherited a good side who had been used to winning and he was well respected by his colleagues; the Middlesex Committee too were fully behind him. Under Gatting, the county showed no sign of lowering the standards which they had attained under Brearley.

In his first season as captain, he topped the Middlesex batting averages with 1373 runs at an average of 72.26. He added 318 with Clive Radley for the third wicket against the New Zealanders at Lord's, going on to score 216. At the end of the summer, he was named as one of Wisden's 'Five Cricketers of the Year' – a great achievement.

On his way to the wicket, Mike Gatting is quite a formidable sight; the swirling of the arms and bat and on arrival at the crease, a most emphatic stance – he is along with Graham Gooch and Ian Botham (in his heyday!) one of three English born batsmen capable of completely destroying the opposition attack.

He topped the national batting averages in 1984, scoring 2150 runs for Middlesex at 71.66, though he topped 3000 runs in all matches. He hit the highest score of his career this season, 258 against Somerset at Bath. His innings lasted 276 minutes and contained 8 sixes and 32 fours and was the highest score made for the county since Jack Robertson's 331 not out in 1949. The season also saw him hit a couple of Sunday League centuries, 109 v Leicestershire at Grace Road and 103 not out v Surrey at the Oval.

By this time, he had played in 30 Tests for England, but couldn't reproduce his Middlesex form in international cricket. Indeed it wasn't until his fifth overseas tour to India at the end of the 1984 season that he really established a secure place in England's middle order. On that tour to India, he was made vice-captain, his bulldog attitude proving an excellent foil to David Gower. He had wreaked havoc on all county attacks, yet it was his 54th Test innings before he scored his first hundred. He hit 136 at Bombay and then his highest ever Test score, 207 at Madras.

In 1985, he hit a glorious unbeaten 143 against Sussex at Hove in the Benson and Hedges Cup, following it in 1986 with 118 not out against Northamptonshire in the Nat West Trophy – thus completing centuries in all the one-day competitions.

In 1986, he became captain of England, making it difficult for him to return to the county for odd games in between Tests and produce a sparkling century to order, though he did score 452 runs (Average 50.22) to head the Middlesex batting averages.

He led England's quest to retain the Ashes in 1986-87, which they did successfully, becoming the third England captain to retain the Ashes in Australia.

He returned for the 1987 season to once again top the Middlesex batting averages and take two hundreds, 124 (at Edgbaston) and 124 (at the Oval) off the Pakistani attack in the Test series. On the tour to Pakistan in 1987-88, he found the intrigue of Pakistani cricket totally unacceptable and was involved in the Shakoor Rana incident.

In 1988, he hit another double hundred for Middlesex, 210 against Nottinghamshire at Lord's; it was also the season that he was relieved of the England captaincy during the visit of the West Indies for a supposed bit of light-hearted dalliance with a barmaid. It was also his benefit season, raising £205,000 – the figure is a record for any benefit, over £50,000 more than Graham Gooch's £153,906 the previous highest.

He has played in 68 Tests and has scored 3870 runs for an average of 37.57.

After topping the Middlesex batting averages in 1989, he had to settle for second place behind Desmond Haynes in 1990. An exciting batsman to watch and bold in his approach, he scored 1685 runs at an average of 58.10. His highest score was 170 not out against Somerset, Gatting hitting 6 fours in one Ian Swallow over. He also hit a magnificent 119 not out from 209 (the next highest scorer was John Emburey with 14) on a terrible Derby wicket, reported to Lord's as unfit after inspection by TCCB officials. He also showed against Kent that he hadn't lost his ability with the ball, ending their innings with 4 for 0 in 7 balls to finish with 4 for 2.

I recall David Hughes, Lancashire's mercurial leader commenting last season that Gatting's decision to put Brown on for the antepenultimate over against Gloucestershire (40 to win with 3 wickets left and 18 coming off Brown's over) was 'a great piece of captaincy.' Though the tabloid press branded the affair a farce!

Though out of the England set-up at present for his part in the last unnoficial South African tour affair, Michael William Gatting remains a powerful influence in English cricket.

NIGEL HAIG

Born: 12 December 1887. Kensington
Died: 27 October 1966
Played: 1912–1934

FIRST-CLASS MIDDLESEX RECORDS

Matches	*Innings*	*NO*	*Runs*	*HS*	*Ave*	*1OOs*
417	630	39	12289	131	20.79	11

Runs	*Wkts*	*Ave*	*Best*	*5wI*	*Ct*
24264	931	26.06	7-33	41	182

TEST MATCHES: 5

Nigel Esme Haig was a nephew of Lord Harris, which obviously gave him a most useful start in his cricketing life, though it took some time for his own talents to develop. At Eton, he couldn't get into the first XI and he didn't go to University.

He made his Middlesex debut in 1912, as a hard-hitting batsman and tearaway fast bowler. He averaged 24 with the bat and shared in an unbeaten stand of 158 with F T Mann for the fifth wicket against Kent at Maidstone. He was used primarily as a batsman, his one wicket that season costing him 101 runs.

During the First World War, he served with the Royal Field Artillery and was awarded the MC. After the war years, his fast-medium bowling improved out of all recognition and he played an important role in Middlesex's two Championship winning sides.

In 1920, he hit the highest of his 11 centuries for Middlesex, 131 against Sussex at Lord's. In fact, the first four Middlesex batsmen to score hundreds that day. He reached his century in an hour and a half, outpacing J W Hearne who was batting in his usual faultless style. When Haig was dismissed off the bowling of Tate, he had helped to add 228 for the third wicket. This season also saw him score a quickfire 86 against Yorkshire on a sticky Bradford wicket. Later that summer he produced his best figures with the ball in the match against Kent at Canterbury. He scored 57 as the county side struggled to reach 212. It was in this match that Haig as the second batsman dismissed by 'Titch' Freeman in his hat-trick. When Kent went in to bat, Haig used the soft pitch to full advantage, taking 7 for 14 off just 37 balls (eventually finishing with 7 for 33) as Middlesex won a close game by 5 runs.

As a bowler, he had immense stamina and could maintain a nagging accuracy for long spells. He and Durston in 1921, were probably the best pair of opening bowlers in the country, after Yorkshire's Macaulay and Waddington.

As in the previous season, the fixture against Surrey was the all-important one. Whereas in 1920 Middlesex had to win to take the Championship title, in 1921 they only had to draw. Haig's fast swing bowling gave Middlesex a fighting chance, as he took 5 for 62 from 23.2 overs to help dismiss Surrey in their second innings for 184, Middlesex going on to win by six wickets.

He did the 'double' for the first time this season and played for England against Australia in the second disastrous Test series and then made four appearances against the West Indies for the on F S G Calthorpes MCC team of 1929-30, though without achieving much success – a top score of 47 at Bridgetown and 3 for 73 at Kingston.

As a batsman, his style could not be classed as classic. His unorthodox batting was suspect to pace bowling, but he could certainly hit the ball with surprising power and twice hit hundreds before lunch.

In 1924, in the match against Gloucestershire at Packer's Ground, Bristol, he bowled brilliantly to take 6 for 11 from 12 overs as the West Country side were shot out for 31, ably supported by Durston (4 for 18), yet surprisingly, Gloucestershire went on to win the match by 61 runs, as Charlie Parker, the left-arm spinner accomplished the hat-trick twice. The following season, Haig shared in a second ninth wicket stand for the Gentlemen against the Players with Gubby Allen at the Oval.

In 1928, Nigel Haig took over the captaincy and because Lee was now without a regular opening partner, he often went in first with him. He had done the 'double' twice before, but in 1929 he achieved the targets with reasonable ease, ending with 1552 runs and 129 wickets. Exactly 100 of his wickets that season came in championship matches. He showed his worth to the side against Worcestershire this season as an opening batsman and opening bowler. He made 130 out of an opening stand of 175 in 2 hours and had match figures of 7 for 126.

As a captain, Haig came to the position at a time when the county were going through a bad period and the best he could do was to keep the county going. I'm sure no captain worked harder for his side, even at the time, he was well into his forties. He probably over bowled himself, though he was probably unaware; his batting lost nothing of its daring, he still remained a great trier.

In 1931, he added 200 with Patsy Hendren for the fifth wicket against Nottinghamshire at Trent Bridge. He was a dashing driver and great cutter of the ball, probably scoring the greater proportion of his runs with hits to the boundary. In 1932, Haig soldiered gamely on, scoring only 552 runs and capturing 33 wickets – though he did play in all 28 matches. This was his last year of captaincy on his own, sharing it with H J Enthoven the following season.

In his last game in charge against Nottinghamshire, there were problems. The bowling of Bill Voce led Middlesex to launch an enquiry and they threatened never to play Nottinghamshire again. Haig commented that Voce after bowling fairly initially, carried out a 'direct and consistent attack on the batsman'.

Nigel Haig retired in October 1934, the Middlesex Committee paying public tribute to him; ending with: 'His untiring energy both in bowling and fielding and good nerve when things have been going wrong, have been a great example to the eleven'. He helped to encourage the young players that were to take the County near to success the following few years.

Later, he married the successful stage actress, Unity Moore, who had played Peter Pan in the West End of London. With financial backing from his uncle Lord Harris, Nigel Haig could afford to play for over 20 years, whilst he filled his winters with gentlemanly pursuits that included private cricket tours as well as other games at which he excelled, such as real tennis, racquets, squash and golf.

When he was appearing for the MCC, he put in for such high expenses that Sir Francis Lacey ordered one of his minions to return the claim to the Middlesex captain with the suggestion that he might like to have another look at it, 'Oh of course' said Nigel, 'I'm er much obliged', whereupon he promptly amended the expenses form by doubling the amount claimed!

He was a most popular player amongst his fellow-cricketers, often hailed with 'Well done Esmeralda' after an effective piece of cricket.

He died in a Sussex hospital on 27th October 1966 aged 78 – a most celebrated all-round cricketer.

J T HEARNE

Born: 3 May 1867, Chalfont St Giles
Died: 17 April 1944
Played: 1888–1923

FIRST-CLASS MIDDLESEX RECORDS

Matches	*Innings*	*NO*	*Runs*	*HS*	*Ave*	*100s*
453	630	223	4598	65	11.30	0

Runs	*Wkts*	*Ave*	*Best*	*5wI*	*Ct*
38166	2093	18.24	9-32	171	306

TEST MATCHES: 12

John Thomas 'Jack' Hearne came from a famous cricketing family. He was a nephew of both Tom and George Hearne who had played for Buckinghamshire and Middlesex and was a cousin of Alec, Frank and G G Hearne, all players with Kent.

J T began coaching at the Evelyn School ground, where after being seen by Middlesex's A J Webbe, he was asked to play in a Middlesex Colts match and then against the Australians in 1888. He took two wickets at little cost, but unfortunately he couldn't accept the invitation to play in Middlesex's next match against Surrey, one of the masters advising him that he was not qualified. He overcame this difficulty by going to live in

London with his brother, but he still worked at the Evelyn School during the summer months.

In 1890, he received a telegram asking him to play for Middlesex against Nottinghamshire that very same day. When he arrived it was almost lunch and he could see the scoreboard showing 99 for 0, but luckily for him, it was Middlesex that were batting. When Nottinghamshire went into bat, they found young Jack quite a handful, as he went on to take 6 for 62. In his next match after his championship debut, he took the wickets of both WG and E M Grace in the match against Gloucestershire.

In 1891, he took 118 wickets at 10.39 runs apiece in the sixteen games in which he played – he was the first bowler to take 100 wickets in a season for Middlesex and topped the first-class averages. He took 14 for 65 against Yorkshire, but Middlesex still lost; 11 for 47 against Lancashire (including 8 for 22 and four wickets in six balls) and 9 for 32 in a single innings against Nottinghamshire.

In 1891-92, he went to South Africa and though the South African batting at that time was weak, he still did well in claiming 163 wickets at less than 7 runs apiece.

In 1893, he took more wickets for the county than any Middlesex man before him. He took 212 wickets in all matches, but 145 for the county at 16.2 runs each.

As a bowler, he bowled right-hand medium-pace. He had a fairly long run up to the wicket and bowled a perfect length and line. He could vary his pace quite cleverly and was able to send down a very fast delivery that swung with his arm action.

JT bowled over 2000 overs when he topped the averages in 1896, taking 257 wickets at 14.72 runs each, though only 118 of these were for Middlesex. His total has only been exceeded by four bowlers; Hearne reaching his 100th wicket that summer on 12 June, the earliest date that this target had been reached – since equalled by Charlie Parker of Gloucestershire in 1931. He performed the hat-trick against Kent at Tonbridge and in the match against Surrey, took 6 for 26 and 6 for 64.

At Lord's in June, he played a great part as the MCC beat the Australians by an innings. The Aussies were dismissed for 18 (Hearne taking 4 for 4 from 11 overs) and then taking 9 for 73 in their second innings (this was every wicket that fell, for the Australians batted one man short, as Giffen was ill).

In the three Test matches that summer against the Australians, he took 15 wickets at 14.10 runs each. At Lord's he didn't bowl until the second innings when he took 5 for 76 from 36 overs, but at the Oval, he took 6 for 41 and 4 for 19 as England won the decider by 66 runs.

At Hastings, representing the South of England v the Australians, he had figures of:

O	*M*	*R*	*W*
17	13	8	6

He ended the season with 56 wickets in matches against the Australians at 13.17 runs apiece.

In the winter of 1897, he toured Australia with A E Stoddart's team, taking nine wickets in the first Test, the only match England won.

In the eight years up to 1897, he took 1485 first-class wickets at just over 16 runs each. In 1898, he took 129 wickets for Middlesex at 14.64 each, with his best figures being 9 for 68 against Lancashire at Old Trafford (16 for 114 in the match).

The following season, the first occasion that a five match Test series had been played, he set up a record that still remains – that is, the only hat-trick against Australia in a Test match in England. His victims at Headingley are worth noting, Clem Hill, Sidney Gregory and Monty Noble.

Jack Hearne took over 100 wickets in 15 seasons from 1891 to 1904, the only exception being 1901 when he took 99! There seems to be an obvious answer to that rapid decline in his bowling – it was his best year with the bat! Hearne scoring 522 runs at an average of 20.88.

In 1902, he performed the hat-trick against Essex at Lord's, actually taking four wickets in five balls. In 1904, though he usually batted at number 10 or 11, he finished quite high in the national batting averages with 226 runs and an average of 32.28. He was not out 18 times – eight in his first nine and again eight in his last nine innings. In 1907, a strong Lancashire side were dismissed for 84 and 70 with J T Hearne returning match figures of 11 for 67. In 1908, he took 9 for 78 against Yorkshire at Bradford, it seemed it was to be his last great bowling performance.

He made a great come-back in 1910, taking 119 wickets at 12.79 runs apiece, to head the English averages. His length was as perfect as ever, but he had recaptured his quickly controlled off-break that defeated many a top batsman. It caused Plum Warner to comment that he was very nearly in the form of his best days. However, Hearne was now 44 years of age and was bowling on good pitches, far better than he'd encountered some fifteen years ago. It was from 1910 as a first exercise in pitch protection, that the bowler's footholds were covered – this was a great aid to Hearne with his long run-up. One of his best performances that season came against Yorkshire, Hearne demolishing them in their second innings as they chased 185 to win, by taking 6 for 20 (12 for 65 in the match).

In 1911, he was once again the leading wicket-taker with 108 at 18.09 runs each. The following season saw him perform his third hat-trick for Middlesex against Warwickshire at Lord's.

J T Hearne helped to raise the status of professional cricketers by his example. He was certainly a father figure to all young Middlesex and MCC players. He was so widely respected that he was the first professional ever to be elected to the Middlesex Committee in 1920.

In 1923, he played for Middlesex one more time at Edinburgh, taking 6 for 64 against Scotland.

Playing so often at Lord's, he took 1719 wickets there; more than any other man. He took more first-class wickets, 3061 than any man bar Rhodes, Freeman and Parker and probably would have taken more if he'd started before he was 23.

On his retirement, he became a much respected coach, many of his years devoted to Oxford in The Parks. He also spent six winters in the employment of the Maharaja of Patiala in India.

He died on 17th April 1944, one of the greatest fast-medium bowlers of all-time.

JOHN W HEARNE

Born: 11 February 1891, Hillingdon
Died: 14 September 1965
Played: 1909–1936

FIRST-CLASS MIDDLESEX RECORDS

Matches	*Innings*	*NO*	*Runs*	*HS*	*Ave*	*100s*
465	744	73	27612	285*	41.15	71

Runs	*Wkts*	*Ave*	*Best*	*5wI*	*Ct*
33309	1438	23.16	9-61	88	240

TEST MATCHES: 24

John William Hearne was a member of the most famous of cricket families, his cousin JT also playing for Middlesex.

He joined the Lord's ground-staff as a 15 year old matchcard boy in 1906, receiving his first trial for the county some three years later; creating quite an impression with his knock of 71 against Somerset at Taunton.

In 1910, he hit two centuries and began to bowl with much more success. His maiden first-class century, 155, was made against Somerset, Hearne following this with 5 for 28 in Somerset's second innings to give his side victory. He hit 108 against Sussex and at Lord's in August, he took seven Essex wickets in 25 balls, without conceding a run. He ended the season with 725 runs and 48 wickets.

The following season he scored 1447 runs and took 87 wickets. He hit 234 not out against Somerset at Lord's and took 9 for 82 against Surrey, also on his home ground. He also performed the hat-trick against Essex (his other hat-trick was also against Essex in 1922). He was just 20 years of age and was named as one of Wisden's Five Cricketers of the Year.

He began his Test career in 1911-12 after Plum Warner had pressed his claims when some members of the Middlesex Committee considered him too young to tour Australia. Yet it was on this tour, that he hit his only Test century, 114 at Melbourne – the youngest batsman (20 years 324 days) to score a hundred for England until Denis Compton hit his in 1938.

In 1913, he scored 1663 runs at an average of 51.97 and captured 107 wickets at a cost of 22.04 runs apiece. His top score that season was 189 made in 4 hours in the match against Hampshire at Southampton.

In 1914, he hit 2021 runs at an average of 74.85 to head the national batting averages. He hit eight centuries and also took 114 wickets at 21.42 each. When Middlesex played Essex at Leyton, Hearne scored 106 not out and took 7 for 54 and 7 for 92, as Middlesex won by an innings and 56 runs after declaring their first innings at 464 for 1. He scored 204 against Lancashire at Lord's and 191 not out against Surrey at the Oval to become the first man to score 2000 runs for Middlesex alone.

When cricket resumed after the war, he scored 218 not out against Hampshire at Lord's as he and Patsy Hendren added 325 for the fourth wicket to establish the Middlesex record.

As a middle-order batsman with a straight bat in defence, he accumulated many runs by masterful placement of the ball, particularly on the leg-side. He could hit hard and once lifted the ball over the boundary ropes for six off three successive deliveries, although he rarely attempted hits like that, preferring to keep the ball on the ground.

He began as a leg-break bowler of the experimental type, adding control of length to his spin after his initial season. Later in his career, he relied more on variations of flight and speed and the occasional off-break. Hearne possessed sharp powers of spin and that dip in the flight that separates the best from the average. Utilising two slips and a gully on a dusty track, he was as dangerous as anyone.

In 1920 he scored 1638 runs (Average 54.60) and captured 123 wickets (at 18.22 each) in the county championship. In all matches that season, he scored 2148 runs (Average 55.07) and took 142 wickets (17.83 each) —it was his best season. He was second only to Hobbs, yet after illness and injury, he made about 500 runs less than would have been possible if he had been fit throughout the season.

Many of his feats that season went a long way in helping the county win the title. At Canterbury, Kent only wanted 123 in the last innings to win the match. They started well, but Hearne came on and took 8 for 26 in 16 overs, Middlesex winning by 5 runs. At the Oval against Surrey, he scored 178 and had match figures of 9 for 101. He batted five minutes short of an entire day to score his 178 when the next highest score was 40; he also scored an unbeaten 215 against Warwickshire at Edgbaston to begin a long series of successes on that ground.

In 1921, he hit a double hundred, 202, for the second successive year against Warwickshire at Edgbaston and one of the best innings of his career, hitting an unbeaten 175 from a total of 289 against Yorkshire.

He continued his remarkable form against Warwickshire at Edgbaston in 1922 with another double century, 221 not out; he also hit 201 not out against Gloucestershire.

In 1923, he missed over a month's cricket at the end of the season, yet still scored 1252 runs (Average 46.37) and took 103 wickets (at 19.48 each). It was during this season that he took part for the second time in establishing a quite unique record – the first four men in the Middlesex batting line-up all scoring centuries. Hearne's score on this occasion was 232 as he and Hendren added 375 for the third wicket against Hampshire at Southampton. This stood as a world record for eleven years and was a Middlesex record until 1948. At Lord's in the match against Sussex, he scored 140 and 57 not out and took 6 for 83 and 6 for 45. However, in the return game at Hove, he had his right hand broken by a delivery from Gilligan and couldn't play again that summer.

His Test career came to a sudden end in 1926 when he was dropped after neither batting nor bowling in the Trent Bridge Test.

In 1927, he started the season in such good form, that he made 750 runs in May and they included an innings of 245 not out against Gloucestershire at Bristol. Also this season, he turned in a fine all-round performance in the match against Surrey at Lord's. He scored 167 not out and took 8 for 39 in Surrey's first innings, yet Middlesex still lost by 5 wickets.

He hit the last of his 11 double centuries for Middlesex against Essex at Leyton in 1929, this was his highest score, 285 not out. In 1931, he scored hundreds in both innings, 104 and 101 not out against Glamorgan at Lord's and carried his bat for 152 not out from Middlesex's total of 390 against Leicestershire at Grace Road. In 1932, he found something of his old form and scored 2151 runs at an average of 44. The following summer saw him return the best bowling figures of his career when he took 9 for 61 against Derbyshire at Chesterfield.

In all first-class matches, he scored 37,252 runs with 96 centuries and took 1839 wickets. His record speaks for itself, but it is all the more remarkable when one considers a break of four years during the war, his slight physique and a record of illness and injury that forced him to miss many matches. At his best, Hearne only had one rival as an all-rounder and that was Kent's Frank Woolley.

In his later years, he ran his sports shop in Ealing and coached at indoor cricket schools.

Playing until he was 45 years old, he was a wonderful allround cricketer of great talent and distinction.

PATSY HENDREN

Born: 5 February 1889, Turnham Green
Died: 4 October 1962
Played: 1907–1937

FIRST-CLASS MIDDLESEX RECORDS

Matches	*Innings*	*NO*	*Runs*	*HS*	*Ave*	*100s*
581	928	119	40302	301*	48.82	119

Runs	*Wkts*	*Ave*	*Best*	*5wI*	*Ct*
2065	39	52.95	5-43	1	562

TEST MATCHES: 51

Elias 'Patsy' Hendren was born at Turnham Green on 5 February 1889, one of six children of Irish parents, both of whom were dead by the time he was 14. At the age of 15, Patsy was playing for Turnham Green. It was at about the same time that the great Middlesex bowler J T Hearne brought over a side to play the local team; Patsy impressing against the ageing Tom Richardson of Surrey, on an uneven Chiswick Park wicket.

He soon followed his elder brother, Denis to Lord's and was selling scorecards and bowling in the nets for hours against the rich MCC members. He opened the innings for the Middlesex 2nd XI against Kent at Lord's in May 1906, scoring 13 in each innings. In those early days, his fielding impressed Plum Warner so much, that Patsy was given his Middlesex debut for the game against Lancashire at Lord's in 1907. Hendren's first game turned out to be an historic one. Only 57 runs were scored on the first day and on the second, the spectators were so displeased with the delay caused by the previous day's rain, that they assembled in front of the pavilion and one or two walked on the pitch. Archie MacLaren, the Lancashire captain, then refused to continue the match, saying that the wicket had been damaged beyond repair. Hendren thus had to wait until 1908 before playing his first innings. It has to be said though, that he didn't fulfil Warner's expectations in the years up to the outbreak of World War One.

In his younger days, he was a notable wing forward for Brentford, Queen's Park Rangers, Manchester City and Coventry City and in 1919, he appeared in a 'Victory' international against Wales.

In 1919, with the return of peace, he soared to second place in the first-class list with 1655 runs and an average of 61.29. His top score that season was 201 made against Hampshire at Lord's, as he and J W Hearne added 325 to set a new Middlesex fourth wicket record.

He had a great year in 1920, scoring 2520 runs and averaging 61 again, to top the England averages. Perhaps more important than the number of runs was the way they were made. Against Nottinghamshire at Lord's he hit 232 – the last 182 coming in an hour and three quarters. His 158 against Warwickshire took him less than two and a half hours. In 1920-21, he toured Australia with England, scoring fifties in each of the first three Tests he played.

In 1921, his bat couldn't go wrong in the first few weeks of the season. In consecutive innings for Middlesex, he scored 49, 107, 2, 102, 60, 56, 34, 72, 40 and 52 (v Warwick Armstrong's Australians). He was rightly chosen for the first Test at Trent Bridge, where he was dismissed clean bowled by a thunder-bolt of a ball from Gregory – Ted McDonald bowled him for 7 in the second innings. He ended the season with 2095 runs and an average of 69.83, but seemed nervous on the big occasions, scoring just 17 runs in 4 innings for England against Australia.

He headed the first-class batting averages again in both 1922 and 1923, setting a Middlesex record in the latter, with 2669 runs at an average of 83.40. It was in 1923 that he put on 375 with J W Hearne for the third wicket against Hampshire at Southampton – it was a world record at the time.

When he was picked in representative matches, Patsy became desperately nervous, especially at the start of his innings. Yet after the series against South Africa in 1924, he began to overcome this problem and became more or less a regular middle-order batsman in the England side. In that series against South Africa, he scored 132 at Headingley and 142 at the Oval.

He was christened Elias, but as he looked Irish, his team-mates called him Pat and his close friends 'Murphy'. Whilst Jack Hearne his partner in many stands called him 'Spud', he was known as 'Patsy' to the crowd.

In 1925, he scored 2006 runs at an average of 60.78 with three double centuries. He hit 234 Worcestershire at Lord's, and 240 v Kent at Tonbridge. He also hit an unbeaten 206 against Nottinghamshire at Trent Bridge, when Middlesex were set to get 502 and got the runs in 6 hour 15 minutes. He and F T Mann hit the last 271 runs in 195 minutes.

The following season saw him score his first Test hundred against Australia, 127 at Lord's and a magnificent 213 against Yorkshire to save the match.

Patsy's sense of humour was both uncomplicated and good natured. Walter Robins always played the spinners by getting down the wicket to either drive them or play a defensive shot if he couldn't; if he missed his defensive shot, he would carry on walking to the pavilion. When Middlesex were playing Derbyshire at Derby, he played such a shot against Tommy Mitchell's leg-spin, missed it and carried on his way. Patsy at the non-strikers end shouted 'He's missed it, get back' Robins spun round and did a spectacular dive into his crease, only to find the Derbyshire wicketkeeper and slip fielders in conversation and the bails lying on the ground!

One of Patsy's favourite tricks was to chase after the ball, stop, appear to pick it up and stand there. The batsman would then hesitate over taking another run, for they couldn't be sure whether the ball was in his hand or many yards past him.

Alf Gover, the Surrey and England quick bowler told the story of when he was a young enthusiastic bowler in 1928 Patsy asked him if he was fast, to which Gover replied that he was. 'Well go easy on me said Patsy, I'm getting on and you might hit me.' When Patsy came in to bat he had three balls to face from Gover. All were short-pitched, the first was hooked for four, the second to the third man boundary and the third hooked for six. When Jack Hobbs asked Gover what he was playing at, he told him what Patsy had said. Hobbs burst out laughing, telling him that Patsy was the best hooker in the world. He ended that 1928 season with 311 runs in all matches with an average of 70.44.

Perhaps his best innings in top-class cricket was his 169 against Australia at Brisbane in the first Test of the 1928-29 rubber – an innings which took England from a moderate score with five men out to a handsome victory by 675 runs after two Australian batting failures. In 1929, he hit 116 not out in Middlesex's total of 154 against Yorkshire at Bradford. On a drying wicket, he destroyed Wilfred Rhodes, one of the best bowlers of all time.

On the 1929-30 England tour of the West Indies, he established himself as the number one folk hero. He scored 1766 runs at an average of 126.14 (including four double hundreds) on the tour and 693 runs in the Test series at an average of 115.50. He scored 223 not out and 211 not out in successive games against Barbados, 205 not out in the second Test and 254 not out off the British Guiana attack. His centuries in the second match with British Guiana and the third Test seem but trifles by comparison. On the hard West Indian wickets, he hooked and pulled all the bowlers with great regularity. One of his best loved tricks on that tour was to creep in close on the legside as the bowler was running in, the West Indian spectators would shout, 'Watch dat man; Watch dat Patsy!' the batsman would turn round and Patsy would make much of being rumbled. The affection for him developed into almost a cult and West Indian streets and children irrespective of sex, were christened Patsy'.

As Neville Cardus once wrote; Patsy's smile on the field as well as off it, was so wide, that he often expected he would one day be given out 'Smile before wicket.'

Hendren once threw in an apple instead of the ball and reputedly broke the wickets! His popularity was only a part of his greatness, but it is a quality which will never be forgotten.

In 1931, he emulated his feat of some eleven years earlier, by scoring 232 against Nottinghamshire, this time at Trent Bridge, to finish the season with 241 runs at an average of 58.82.

In 1933, he caused something of a sensation at Lord's when he batted against the West Indies fast bowlers, wearing a special cap. It had three peaks, two covered the ears and temples and was lined with sponge rubber – it had been fashioned by his wife. He scored five centuries in six consecutive innings – 111, 101, 101, 12, 105, 154 and hit the highest score of his career, 301 not out for Middlesex in their match against Worcestershire at Dudley. At the time, this was the best ever score for Middlesex in first-class cricket and wasn't beaten until Jack Robertson scored 331 not out against the same county some sixteen years later. Hendren ended the season with 3186 runs in all matches and qualified for his third benefit at the age of 44, a unique compliment in Middlesex history.

In 1934 at the age of 45 years 151 days, he became the second oldest batsman after J B Hobbs to score a Test century – in fact, he took three hundreds off the Australians and their great bowler O'Reilly that season, the other two for Middlesex.

After a rather traumatic start to his Test career, he ended with 51 appearances and 3525 runs, averaging 47.64.

He was a thrilling batsman, with a marvellous eye, supple wrists and dazzling footwork. He had all the shots, playing the pull and the hook magnificently. He was without doubt, one of the finest batsmen in the period between the two wars.

In his last season in 1937 at the age of 48, he scored 1809 runs, being able to delight the crowd with both his batting ability and comic fun. When asked why he was retiring, he replied 'While you can still say why, rather than when.' Towards the end of his career, he was joined in the Middlesex side by Bill Edrich and Denis Compton, two youngsters who shared Patsy's view of cricket being a game of fun. Both learned a great deal from Patsy in their early days.

In his last game at Lord's and his last in the County Championship, he scored 103 against Surrey – 17,000 spectators giving him a great reception. The crowd stopped play for a whole five minutes by singing 'For he's a jolly good fellow.' There has never been a more genuine tribute. He did return to play for England Past and Present against Sir Pelham Warner's XI in the 1938 Hastings Festival,

On his retirement, he succeeded Wilfred Rhodes as coach at Harrow School and in 1939, Harrow beat Eton for the first time since 1908. He retired from Harrow in 1947 and for four years held a similar post with Sussex. He was elected a life member of the MCC in 1949 and also served on the Middlesex Committee. In 1952, he became Middlesex's scorer, continuing until he was forced to give it up due to ill-health in 1959.

His achievements are many; only Hobbs and Woolley have passed his total of 57611 runs and only Hobbs has scored more than his 170 centuries. Only Wally Hammond has scored more runs in a decade and in the twenties, Patsy scored 28711 more than anyone else. He hit 22 double centuries during his career, only Sir Don Bradman (37) and W R Hammond (36) have hit more. On four occasions he scored a century in each innings of the same match, a feat bettered only by W R Hammond (7) Sir Jack Hobbs (6) and C B Fry (5).

Patsy Hendren is not a player who is remembered primarily for his achievements and runs scored, but rather for the pleasure that his sense of fun and generous spirit brought to the game.

RON HOOKER

Born: 22 February 1935, Lower Clapton
Played: 1956–69

FIRST-CLASS MIDDLESEX RECORDS

Matches	*Innings*	*NO*	*Runs*	*HS*	*Ave*	*100s*
300	442	71	8222	137	22.16	5

Runs	*Wkts*	*Ave*	*Best*	*5wI*	*Ct*
13957	490	27.46	7-18	16	302

TEST MATCHES: 0

When he first joined Middlesex, Ron Hooker was thought of as solely a batsman, though he later developed into a medium-paced seam bowler of great value as first change and his aggressive batting dropped off somewhat.

He enjoyed a most lively County Championship debut at Chesterfield in May 1956. The young all-rounder scored a well-hit 77 and took the early wickets of Derbyshire batsmen Kelly and Smith to complete a most satisfactory debut.

Hooker was a superb fielder, making the backward short-leg position his own by right of brilliance.

His whirlwind batting continued, hitting 91 in quickfire time against Nottinghamshire as Middlesex totalled 397 for 9 declared. In 1959, when Middlesex played Kent at Gravesend, he hit the highest score of his career, 137. His innings contained three sixes and 26 fours (122 in boundaries).

After John Warr's departure at the end of the 1960 season, Ron Hooker was used more and more as a stock bowler, having a successful summer in 1961 with 67 wickets and 38 catches. One of his best performances that season was his 5 for 30 against Surrey at Lords. His analysis included a spell of 4 for 6 in 14 balls with the wickets of Barrington, May, Constable and Willett.

In 1965, Hooker was the leading wicket-taker for the county with 86 wickets in the championship alone – it was his best season with the ball. His best figures that summer were 7 for 24 against Hampshire at Lord's as they were bowled out for 83.

In 1966, he continued to bowl well, but had a day to remember with the bat on a crumbling wicket at Weston-super-Mare. When he went in, Middlesex were 110 for 5; Ron Hooker proceeded to hit 102 out of 120 and Middlesex went on to win the match easily – his hundred came up in 87 minutes. This was also the season in which Hooker was first troubled by a back injury which was to force him to retire three years later.

Like other Middlesex players who had to retire during that period, Ron Hooker I'm sure would have been an outstanding one-day player. One of his last performances in Middlesex colours was in a John Player League fixture against Surrey at Lord's – the men from the Oval were dismissed for 83, with Hooker taking six wickets for 6 runs!

HARRY LEE

Born: 26 October 1890, Marylebone
Died: 21 April 1981
Played: 1911–1934

FIRST-CLASS MIDDLESEX RECORDS

Matches	*Innings*	*NO*	*Runs*	*HS*	*Ave*	*100s*
401	666	45	18594	243*	29.94	23

Runs	*Wkts*	*Ave*	*Best*	*5wI*	*Ct*
11064	340	32.54	8-39	7	164

TEST MATCHES: 1

Born at Marylebone, Harry Lee used to work in his father's greengrocer's shop, delivering and collecting early in the morning. He was literally a product of street cricket, engaged as a ground-boy at Lord's when he was sixteen. He was regarded mainly as a useful slow bowler, but made his debut for Middlesex in 1911 as a batsman.

He didn't have too much success, but on the outbreak of the First World War, several amateur players joined the forces and Lee got his chance. He took it, with a superb innings of 139 against Nottinghamshire.

At the end of the season, he too joined up and in May 1915 was reported killed in action. Fortunately the report wasn't true, he had in fact broken his thigh badly and had been taken a prisoner by the Germans. He was repatriated a few months later, with one leg shorter than the other and told he would never play cricket again. However, Harry Lee proved the specialists wrong, for by the summer of 1916, he was playing for the MCC against school sides and scoring runs. He also spent some eighteen months in India, coaching and playing for the Maharajah of Cooch Behar. In fact, he had recovered so much, that few people would have guessed that he'd been wounded.

When the first-class game resumed in 1919, he soon established himself in the Middlesex XI, scoring 163 and 126 in the match against Surrey at the Oval.

In 1920, when Middlesex won the Championship, he made another hundred against the strong Surrey side at the Oval. At Southampton, he hit the first double century (221 not out) of his career. Against Sussex that season, he scored 119 as he and Warner put on 241 for the first wicket; he also had match figures of 11 for 68 (5 for 21 and 6 for 47) as Middlesex won by an innings and 130 runs. He was one of four Middlesex batsmen to score a hundred in this match; strangely enough, the only time it has been equalled was by Middlesex in 1923 against Hampshire at Southampton when Lee was again one of the four centurions.

He ended the 1920 season with 1473 runs (Average 44.63) and took 40 wickets at a cost of 24 runs each, thus becoming a serious contender for the MCC side to tour Australia.

In 1921 he hit the highest score of his career, an unbeaten 243 against Northamptonshire at Lord's, helped when G E V Crutchley put on 231 with him for the first wicket. Generally speaking though, he was less successful with the bat. However, he had his best season with the ball, taking 72 wickets in all matches at 19.66 runs each. When he took 6 for 53 against the Australians, his victims included Ryder, Andrews, Armstrong and Gregory.

His best figures with the ball were 8 for 39 against Gloucestershire at Cheltenham in 1923.

Harry Lee was the ideal county player, a born fighter. In 1924, he carried his bat for 52 not out from 132 against Essex at Lord's and in the match against Gloucestershire in which Middlesex lost by 61 runs, only Harry Lee (21 in both innings) was to reach double figures in each innings.

In 1928, he returned to something like his old form with the bat, averaging 41.64. He represented the Players against the Gentlemen once only at the Oval that season, when he hit a half century.

In 1929 against Surrey, he and Gubby Allen (155) put on 319 for the second wicket in the match at the Oval, Lee going on to make 225. He hit another double hundred that summer, 200 against Oxford University. He also hit two centuries in the same match, 124 and 105 not out for the second time against Lancashire at Lord's.

As a batsman, Harry Lee had an exaggerated crouch at the wicket and favoured the leg-side. He bowled slow-medium off-spinners and could also make the ball float away. He occasionally took the new ball, getting plenty of pace off the wicket and was able to keep a good length.

He often spent the winter months coaching in South Africa and it was there that he was co-opted by Percy Chapman's MCC side in 1930-31 after Andrew Sandham had been injured in a car accident. He made his one and only Test appearance at Johannesburg in the fourth Test Match he opened with R E S Wyatt scoring 18 and 1.

Two of his brothers, Frank and Jack played for Somerset and at Lord's in 1933, the score card for that particular match read in Middlesex's first innings: H W Lee ct. F S Lee bowled J W Lee 82.

In 1934, he was dropped from the Middlesex XI in an effort to encourage the younger members of the Club, but he showed that there was still plenty of cricket left in him, with a hundred for the MCC against Oxford University and another for Middlesex in late August against Warwickshire when he was recalled for a couple of matches.

He was a little slow on his feet, due to the war wound and with his modern-day two-eyed stance, he was a solid and most dependable cricketer, always giving of his best.

From 1935 to 1946 he was a first-class umpire and from 1949 to 1953 he was coach at Downside. He also turned his hand to writing, being the author of *Forty Years of English Cricket*.

He died in hospital after a long illness, on 21 April 1981 in his 91st year. He was at the time of his death, the second oldest surviving Test cricketer, Andrew Sandham being the elder by three months.

GREGOR MacGREGOR

Born: 31 March 1869, Merchiston
Died: 20 August 1919
Played: 1992–1907

FIRST-CLASS MIDDLESEX RECORDS

Matches	*Innings*	*NO*	*Runs*	*HS*	*Ave*	*100s*
184	286	39	4846	141	19.61	2

Runs	*Wkts*	*Ave*	*Best*	*5wI*	*Ct*	*St*
–	–	–	–	–	*280*	*111*

TEST MATCHES: 8

Though born near Edinburgh, Gregor MacGregor moved south with his family and after two years in the Uppingham team, he went up to Cambridge. In the spring of 1888, he was noted as a wicket-keeper of extraordinary ability.

He immediately gained his Blue, though the match with Oxford was drawn, even a fourth day was of no use in that dreadful summer.

Cambridge had had Alfred Lyttleton behind the stumps, but even his warmest admirers, including A G Steel, had to admit that MacGregor was the better of the two.

Throughout his career at Cambridge, he was associated with Australian-born Sammy Woods, who was later to play for both Australia and England and to make a name for himself with Somerset. Woods and MacGregor struck up a fine partnership. Woods in those days was the fastest amateur bowler in England and one that terrorised the Oxford batsmen. MacGregor had very strong claims to being England's best amateur wicket-keeper of all time, for the fashion of standing back had not then become general and so standing up to the wicket, MacGregor's fearless skill enabled him to cope with every emergency, for Woods was apt to be a little erratic when pitching the ball.

After that wet summer of 1888, Cambridge had three successive years of victory against the Dark Blues. Woods was captain in 1890 and MacGregor the following season.

In 1890, he contributed 131 to the highest second innings total in Britain, 703 for 9 declared by Cambridge University in the match against Sussex at Hove. Also that season, playing against the Australians at Lord's while still an undergraduate, he allowed no byes in either innings.

In 1891-92, he toured Australia with Lord Sheffield's team, it was the only time that he didn't do himself justice – the Australian critics expected a lot more, but he disappointed and was not up to his usual high standard.

He made his Middlesex debut in July 1892 coming into the side from Cambridge for the Lancashire match at Old Trafford. He was just 23, yet he was already a Test cricketer and a Scottish International Rugby player.

He represented the University in Varsity matches in 1889 and 1890 and was also chosen in that first year to play in all Scotland's matches that season. He played both at full-back and centre, ranking with the foremost of rugby men of his day. His last international appearance (he won 13 caps) was against England at Hampden Park in 1896.

In 1893, he brought a new record to Middlesex with his tally of victims behind the stumps – 29 caught and 5 stumped. Injuries caused him to miss several matches throughout the next few seasons, but in 1897, his hard-hitting brought him his highest score of his career; he was run out for 141 as Middlesex beat Sussex at Lord's by 7 wickets.

After playing in his eight Tests during the nineties, there were reports that his keeping was falling off, but he more than held his own for several more years. In fact, he was appointed captain in 1899, a position he was to hold until 1907. He was a popular and most admirable leader, although he did miss the odd match or two each season.

MacGregor is one of the few cricketers who have made a success of the twin-roles of captain and wicket-keeper. Probably the most difficult position to lead a side from, as the actual wicket-keeping side needs the players' entire concentration. He was a brilliant wicket-keeper, especially in his early years, when he had no other player to touch him save for Lancashire's Pilling. His first season as captain started sensationally as Middlesex defeated Somerset inside 4 hours 15 minutes.

In 1902, he had a really outstanding day at Trent Bridge against

Nottinghamshire. In the Nottinghamshire second innings, he stumped 5 batsmen, including William Gunn and Arthur Shrewsbury, four off the bowling of Bosanquet, the other off Wells.

In 1903, he led Middlesex to their first official county championship. The following season he hit his top score of the summer, 63 not out in a match of modest scoring against Surrey, enabling Middlesex to win by 2 wickets – a fine achievement. His final season was 1907 when he had 34 victims and a batting average of 17 from the 13 matches in which he played. He was replaced by Murrell behind the stumps and P F Warner took over the captaincy.

For some time and up to the end of his life, he was honorary treasurer of the Middlesex County Club.

A hard-hitting batsman and brilliant wicket-keeper, he died on 20 August 1919, a week short of his fiftieth birthday.

GEORGE MANN

Born: 6 September 1917, Byfleet
Played: 1937–1954

FIRST-CLASS MIDDLESEX RECORDS

Matches	*Innings*	*NO*	*Runs*	*HS*	*Ave*	*100s*
54	147	9	3403	116	24.66	3

Runs	*Wkts*	*Ave*	*Best*	*5wI*	*Ct*
45	2	22.50	2-16	0	41

TEST MATCHES: 7

George Mann captained Eton and gained Blues in the last two pre-war years at Cambridge University.

Though making his Middlesex debut in 1937, it was towards the end of the 1939 season when he came into the side at the end of the Cambridge term, that he began to impress. He was a middle-order batsman, keen to play his strokes, especially those on the leg-side. He scored well and fielded brilliantly.

In 1947, he shared with Denis Compton, a stand of 304 for the fourth wicket in Middlesex's match with Surrey at the Oval.

He became captain of Middlesex in 1948 and was both sound and orthodox. Following on from Robins, he probably deliberately avoided experiment. With players like Compton and Edrich missing for all the Tests, he did at least as well as could be expected for anyone succeeding Robins.

Under his leadership, Middlesex were an enterprising side – they only had victory as their sole object.

Mann was a popular captain, an astute leader, modest and a man of generous nature, just like his father. The Middlesex side always wanted to play with Mann and for him. During that 1948 season, he hit a century in Middlesex's innings victory over Nottinghamshire and another against Leicestershire.

His career at this time, followed much the same course as his father's after the First World War. He had also led a championship winning side and an MCC side in South Africa with very much the same results. Both Manns' captained sides who won the Test series and their individual successes were similar too.

In 1948-49, he led his team in South Africa and enabled them to return undefeated after 23 matches. On that tour, he scored 254 runs for an average of 36, compared to father Frank who scored 281 runs at an average of 35. His highest score of 136 not out came in that Test series at Port Elizabeth. Like his father, he was captain of England on all his appearances. He played in 7 Tests, scoring 376 runs for an average of 37.60.

He captained Middlesex for just two seasons, 1948 and 1949, due to the claims of the family brewery. He would also have led England to Australia in 1950-51 but for these claims.

In 1949, he captained the side nobly, leading by example in the field and making runs at a time when they were needed most.

Against New Zealand at Headingley in 1949, his hurricane display of batting saw him hit a vast straight drive on to the Leeds Rugby League ground, via the main stand's roof. His innings of 49 not out came in only 24 minutes, Mann missing the chance of hitting the fastest Test 50 by declaring.

At Lord's in the same series, he created Test history by declaring on the first day – later found to be invalid as the experimental law allowing declarations on the first day of a 3-day match didn't apply to this series.

At the end of the 1949 season, he indicated to the Middlesex Committee that he wouldn't be available on a regular basis in 1950. However, after returning from a trip to South Africa in January 1950, he reluctantly agreed to continue as Middlesex Captain because the County faced a crisis. Within a month though, Mann's business demands had become so great, that he had to confirm that he definitely wouldn't be able to lead the side that summer and so Robins returned.

The 1950 season was effectively the end of his playing career, though he did make occasional appearances in the seasons up to 1954.

Between 1978 and 1983 he was a most accomplished TCCB Chairman and then President of the MCC in 1984–85.

FRANK MANN

Born: 3 March 1888, Winchmore Hill
Died: 6 October 1964
Played: 1909–1931

FIRST-CLASS MIDDLESEX RECORDS

Matches	*Innings*	*NO*	*Runs*	*HS*	*Ave*	*100s*
314	472	39	10656	194	24.61	8

Runs	*Wkts*	*Ave*	*Best*	*5wI*	*Ct*
172	2	86.00	1-15	0	137

TEST MATCHES: 5

Frank Mann's cricket background was a distinguished one. He played in the Malvern XI from 1904 – 07, captaining the side in his last year. He went up to Cambridge, playing in the Varsity matches of 1909, 1910 and 1911, though not producing anything of note.

At Malvern he played soccer, yet at Cambridge he received a Rugby Blue as a forward in 1910.

He made his Middlesex debut in the same season that he went up to Cambridge, beginning with 0 against Lancashire. He played in three games during the month of July that year, his top score being 56 against Somerset. He was soon gaining a reputation as a powerful stroke playing batsman, with a liking for both the on and off drives.

In 1911, he was denied his first century, when he ran out of partners after going in at no 8 and was left stranded on 97 against Surrey, after hitting brilliantly for two and a half hours. In fact, he hit a purple patch towards the end of the season, scoring 356 runs in his last five innings.

His first hundred arrived in 1913 – it was the sort of innings that was to be a feature of Mann's batting (he'd already earned himself a reputation as the Charles Thornton of his day). When he went in to bat, Middlesex were tottering on 39 for 5 against Worcestershire. While 199 runs were added, Mann scored 135 in 165 minutes with two sixes and 18 fours. In fact, he was the last man out after adding 68 for the tenth wicket with Mignon, whose share was 10, Middlesex totalling 238.

That 1913 season saw Mann give some glorious displays of hitting. He began the season with 71 against Sussex at Lord's, but it was the month of August when he excelled. He hit 68 at Southampton, 58 at Eastbourne and then 50 and 71 at Trent Bridge, ending the season with 750 runs.

He joined the XXth Hussars when the hostilities began in 1914, serving with them in France before transferring to the Scots Guards. He was a captain and was severely wounded three times and Mentioned three times in Dispatches. On the last occasion he was wounded, he almost lost his foot. Whilst recovering in Norfolk, he spent much of his time getting himself down to a scratch golfer, yet many thought he would have difficulty in walking after the war. He wasn't as agile as he had been prior to the fighting, but not much got past him at mid-off.

The hit that was considered Mann's best was at Lord's in 1920. Yorkshire's George Macaulay was driven straight on to the covered stands by the sightscreen and then bounced some 20 yards into the Nursery End practice ground. It was hit against the wind and was the longest drive ever seen by Plum Warner. At Hove that same season in the match against Sussex, he hit three sixes off successive balls from Maurice Tate of all bowlers!

Frank Mann was a highly popular man, both on and off the field. He became Middlesex captain in 1921 as the county retained the Championship. He hit two centuries that summer, 112 at Trent Bridge and 101 against Hampshire at Southampton. Against Nottinghamshire, he hit 53 in 19 minutes and was by this time regarded as the biggest hitter in English cricket. Frank Mann was a modest man, making the comment after his Middlesex side had won the Championship that 'the success of the team was due to his predecessor, Plum Warner and the only part he played was tossing the coin'. He held the position until 1928, also acting as honorary secretary.

In 1922, though Middlesex couldn't achieve a third Championship title, Mann had his best season with the bat, scoring 935 runs at an average of 24.60. Essex certainly suffered at Mann's hands. His only hundred for Middlesex came at Leyton when he hit exactly 100 (two sixes and 13 fours) whilst he scored 97 in an hour and a half, despite a bruised hand in the return fixture at Lord's.

He represented the Gentlemen against the Players on 14 occasions between 1914 and 1930 with his best performance coming in 1922; it was at Scarborough, when he hit 82 and 100.

Mann continued to be the scourge of the Yorkshire bowlers and Wilfred Rhodes in particular, hitting him for several sixes at both Lord's and Sheffield. There was a rumpus at Bramall Lane when the teams met in the return fixture, so much so, that Middlesex were determined that they wouldn't play them the following season. That the two committees negotiated and agreed to resolve their differences is due to Frank Mann, the most generous and tactful of men.

In 1925 in the match against Nottinghamshire at Trent Bridge, he helped Middlesex score 502, the highest fourth innings total in the County Championship and beat the midlands side by four wickets. Mann scored 101 as he and Patsy Hendren, who scored 200, hit off the last 271 runs in three and three and quarters of an hour without being separated.

His biggest score was 194 made in five hours (probably his slowest) to help save the game against Warwickshire in 1926. As Wisden commented, 'His best innings were always played in a crisis.'

He continued to lead Middlesex up until 1928 when he was aged 40 and was still entertaining spectators with his big hitting; hitting another of his swashbuckling hundreds against Yorkshire when the white-rose county were challenging for the title. He played in occasional games until 1931 and was a Test selector in 1930 and President of Middlesex.

His decision to stand down was regretted by all. A hard hitting batsman, his importance to Middlesex cricket cannot be judged by figures alone, for he often sacrificed his wicket in the interests of the team.

Frank Mann was 76 when he died suddenly on 6 October 1964 at Milton Lilbourne in Wiltshire.

ALAN MOSS

Born: 14 November, Tottenham
Played: 1950–1963

FIRST-CLASS MIDDLESEX RECORDS

Matches	*Innings*	*NO*	*Runs*	*HS*	*Ave*	*100s*
307	329	141	1234	40	6.56	0

Runs	*Wkts*	*Ave*	*Best*	*5wI*	*Ct*
21566	1088	19.81	8-31	59	121

TEST MATCHES: 9

Born in Tottenham, Alan Moss started his cricketing life as one of the *Evening News* colts. The London evening paper got together some very promising young cricketers and arranged for them to receive coaching and play as a team in several matches.

His enthusiasm for the game was such, that during his National Service in 1950 and 1951, he managed to arrange his RAF duties so that he was available for half of Middlesex's county programme. In 1951, he played in 15 games taking 42 wickets.

He played his first full season after National Service in 1952, taking 95 wickets, 88 of which were in the county championship. He had a similar record the following season and was chosen for the tour of the West Indies, where he played in his first Test at Kingston. He finished second in the West Indies tour averages for all first-class games.

In the first game of the 1954 season, he won the match for Middlesex when they played Worcestershire at Lord's. He took 4 for 54 in their first innings and then bowled unchanged for two and three quarter hours, taking 7 for 101 (11 for 155 in the match). He bowled well in the first half of the season, before a broken bone in the foot (which had long escaped diagnosis) handicapped him.

He took 101 wickets the following summer and then after bowling well in the opening matches of the 1956 season, he was selected for the first Test against Australia at Trent Bridge. He had only bowled 4 overs for 1 run before slipping whilst fielding. He tore his stomach muscles so severely that he missed many matches and only resumed playing again towards the end of the season.

Alan Moss had quite a distinctive bowling action from side-on as he arched back like a bow immediately before he delivered the ball. A tall right-arm fast-medium bowler he was hard-working and capable of bowling long spells, improving his control of line and movement steadily.

In 1956, he performed the hat-trick for the only time in his first-class career against Gloucestershire at Lord's. In 1957, he took 12 for 59 in Middlesex's 231 run win over Kent at Dover.

Although missing 10 matches through Test calls in 1959, he took 73 championship wickets. He was in magnificent form, helping to bowl out Hampshire for 82 in the first match of the season and Glamorgan for 85 in the second.

He had a tremendous season in 1960, taking 114 championship wickets at 12.50 runs each, with a best performance of 8 for 31 against Northamptonshire at Kettering. He was top of the England bowling averages against South Africa with 9 wickets for 138 runs (his best being 4 for 35 at Lord's) and was third in the national bowling averages. However, Moss only played for England when a third seamer could be accommodated. He would surely have played many more times for England, had he not been a contemporary of Trueman, Statham and Tyson. These three limited his appearances for his country to nine.

As a batsman, he could either defend stubbornly or drive over the top, his highest first-class score for Middlesex being 40, whilst at Test level, his 26 against India at Lord's in 1959 was his best. In 1961 he took 112 county championship wickets. He took 8 for 49 against Glamorgan and had match figures of 10 for 95 in the match against Worcestershire at New Road. Halfway through the 1962 season, he took over the captaincy when Bedford was injured and did a fine job, though over the next two years, his form suffered slightly. He was very popular amongst the players and well respected and did a difficult job well.

In 1962, he took 69 wickets, feeling the strain of a lack of support bowler. The following season, he took 79 wickets at 15.92 – he had a fine last season before deciding to retire. He was still a key player at Middlesex and finished his last season as fourth in the national averages.

On his retirement from the game, at the age of 33, he ran a printing business, after taking 1298 first-class wickets.

JOHN MURRAY

Born: 1 April 1935, N. Kensington
Played: 1952–1975

FIRST-CLASS MIDDLESEX RECORDS

Matches	*Innings*	*NO*	*Runs*	*HS*	*Ave*	*100s*
508	761	105	15251	133*	23.25	11

Runs	*Wkts*	*Ave*	*Best*	*5wI*	*Ct*	*St*
134	4	33.50	1-1	0	1024	199

TEST MATCHES: 21

John Murray was born in Notting Hill, the son of a council employee. All his early life centred around the Rugby Boys' Club in Kensington. There were virtually no facilities at school, but the Boys' Club, for whom his father had also played, allowed him to encourage the expression of his twin passions for cricket and soccer.

Famous footballers such as Jimmy Bloomfield and Alan Mullery came from this club and Murray himself had a trial with Arsenal and was offered terms by Brentford.

He was playing in the final of the Boys' Club competition when the Club's wicket-keeper broke a finger. Murray volunteered to take over and within two years found himself in the Middlesex first team. He was accepted on to the Lord's ground staff at the age of 14, but because the school leaving age was raised, he had to stay on at school for another year.

He made his Middlesex debut in 1952 against Leicestershire at Grace Road. Maurice Tompkin, a most delightful cricketer was 14 not out when he advanced well down the pitch to Jim Sims, Murray fumbled the ball giving Tompkin plenty of time to get back – he went on to make a hundred!

The first wicket-keeping coaching he had was when Middlesex arranged for him to have two days' leave in April 1953, so that he could have instruction from Andy Wilson (formerly with Middlesex, but then playing for Gloucestershire). The other coaching he received was from the great Herbert Strudwick who was scoring for Surrey. This was arranged by J Sims who was at the time, Middlesex's scorer. Strudwick came in for three days of the match at 9.30 am to talk to Murray about leg-side work.

From 1953 to 1955, Murray played for a strong RAF side and then at the end of the 1955 season, he took over from Leslie Compton and won his county cap the next year.

In 1956, his first full season, he was the leading wicketkeeper in the country with 77 dismissals (63 caught 14 stumped) – it was the start of the Titmus-Murray combination. The following season, he scored 1025 runs and had 104 dismissals (82 caught 22 stumped), repeating the feat with 102 dismissals in 1960. The only man to beat him, was Kent's Les Ames who did it three times in 1928, 1929 and 1932. He equalled another wicket-keeping record at Lord's in 1967 when in the Test against India, he took six catches in one innings.

After touring New Zealand with the MCC 'A' team in the close season of 1960-61, he made his Test debut in June the following summer at Edgbaston, when England entertained Australia. At Old Trafford in that series, he equalled the England v Australia record of 7 catches in a match. He was often left out of the England team as the selectors followed a policy of including Jim Parks to strengthen the England batting.

John Murray was always immaculately dressed behind the stumps and would go through a studied ritual with his white-backed gloves before settling on his haunches. His gloves would be touched together in front of his face and with hands relaxed and with fingers down would follow a graceful arc before he settled down in readiness for the next delivery.

As a batsman, he was often at his best against fast bowling, both driving and hooking many deliveries to the boundary. Against the slow bowlers, he used his feet to hit beautifully over the top. John Murray was completely relaxed, whether taking the ball, or stroking it wide of mid-on. When he was on form, he made it all look easy.

In 1960, he caught 8 Glamorgan batsmen in the match at Lord's and equalled the feat the following season against Yorkshire (5 caught 3 stumped) also at Lord's.

He was an automatic choice for the tour of Pakistan and India in 1961-62. He did well in Pakistan taking three catches off three different bowlers among the first four wickets to fall in the first Test. However, when he played against India, he conceded 3 byes in the first Test and though he did his utmost, it was revealed that he was suffering from varicose veins and he was flown home. He probably started to play a little too soon in 1962, but was soon reinstated in the Test team.

He went to Australia in 1962-63, under the leadership of Ted Dexter. Surprisingly, Warwickshire's A C Smith kept wicket in the first two Tests, but Murray returned for the third at Sydney. In taking a brilliant leg-side catch off Bill Lawry, he damaged his shoulder and was replaced for the rest of the game by Peter Parfitt. Unfortunately, he received a wrong diagnosis and treatment, which delayed his comeback.

The 1965 season saw Murray play one of his best innings against Yorkshire at Scarborough. Middlesex looked to be set for a good hiding, but Murray's 133 not out turned the tide and saved the day. He also dismissed 9 men in the match at Lord's when Hampshire were the visitors.

In 1966, Murray was recalled for the last Test against the West Indies at the Oval, under Brian Close's leadership. Coming in to bat at 166 for 7, he hit a magnificent 112 in four and a half hours, helping Tom Graveney add 217 for the eighth wicket. In fact, his stylish strokeplay led him to being confused with Graveney in that stand. Also in 1966, he hit another hundred playing for the Rest of the World against a strong pace attack in the Barbados side.

John Murray retired in 1975 at the age of forty. In his last season, he surpassed Herbert Strudwick's record of 1493 dismissals and took it to 1527 (1270 caught 257 stumped). Towards the end of 1975, he was awarded the MBE. His last game for Middlesex was a match I remember well, against Lancashire in the Gillette Cup Final. He only scored 13, but was cheered all the way to the wicket; his one-handed catch to dismiss Frank Hayes was brilliant.

Perhaps the one disappointment was that Middlesex never won anything during his career. After working for Slazenger's he formed his own business with his cousin, known as 'Rodway Security Company'.

He was a Test selector in 1977 and 1978, but he resigned over the choice of Leicestershire's wicket-keeper/batsman for the 1978-79 tour of Australia – a decision he didn't agree with.

He was always an inspiration behind the stumps – it is hard to believe that there was ever a more accomplished wicket-keeper than John Murray.

TIMOTHY O'BRIEN

Born: 5 November 1861, Dublin
Died: 9 November 1948
Played: 1881–1898

FIRST-CLASS MIDDLESEX RECORDS

Matches	*Innings*	*NO*	*Runs*	*HS*	*Avge*	*100s*
156	268	19	7377	202	29.63	10

Runs	*Wkts*	*Ave*	*Best*	*5wI*	*Ct*	*St*
272	2	136.00	1-10	0	111	2

TEST MATCHES: 5

Timothy Carew O'Brien was born in Dublin in 1861 and is probably the most illustrious Irish cricketer.

It must be said though, that O'Brien learnt his cricket in England. He attended a good Catholic School at Downside in Somerset, but it was the move to St Charles College in Notting Hill which allowed him to qualify for Middlesex. It was his performances for the Kensington Park Club that earned him a trial with the county.

He made his Middlesex debut in 1881 at the age of nineteen, but he had little success in those early years, so at the age of twenty two he went to Oxford and New Inn Hall to see if he could score some runs there.

It proved to be remarkably successful for in 1884, O'Brien hit 92 for the University against the Australians, following it with 72 for the MCC against the same opponents. He made his England debut at Old Trafford that season, replacing Lord Harris; O'Brien getting a duck in the first innings and a useful 20 in the second. He did gain a Blue at Oxford, but didn't score a run in either innings of the Varsity match with Cambridge.

He returned to Middlesex to score a fine 119 against Gloucestershire, coupled with some dashing innings against Surrey and topped the batting averages.

In 1885, he married Gunrede Annette Teresa, daughter of Sir Humphrey de Trafford. Cricket must have taken a back seat for a while, as there were two sons and eight daughters of the marriage.In 1886, he became one of the few men to hit a ball clean out of Lord's, playing for the MCC against Rugby School, the ball soaring over the old grandstand.

He played in the opening match of the 1888 season against Yorkshire and then dropped out until mid-July. He returned to play innings of 44, 61,29, 37, 12, 27, 79*, 25, 51*, 59 and 58. Of course in those days, the scale of scoring was much less and 80 so this was a remarkable performance.

Perhaps his greatest moment came in June 1889, when the strong Yorkshire side led by Lord Hawke was at Lord's. On the last afternoon the Yorkshire captain declared, leaving Middlesex 215 minutes in which to score 280 to win the game. With an hour and a half to go and Middlesex on 129 for 4, O'Brien marched to the wicket and with a wonderful display of hitting, destroyed the Yorkshire attack. He had scored 92 in the first innings, but his unbeaten century in 80 minutes in the second, allowed Middlesex to win the game by four wickets with ten minutes to spare. His innings contained 14 fours and six threes.

The Times reported on his innings – 'There was a demonstration in front of the pavilion at the end of the game and cheer after cheer was given for Mr O'Brien. His hitting all round the wicket was of great brilliancy, his precision and skill in timing the ball being most remarkable.'

O'Brien had quite a fiery reputation and in fact, was forced to miss matches against Surrey, because they objected to his attitude. On one occasion, he was batting with Charles Thornton at Harston near Cambridge when he was given out caught after the ball had hit him high on his shirt sleeve. He said to the umpire 'That was either a very ignorant decision or a downright swindle'. To which the umpire replied 'I guess sir, it was just a bit of both.'

He was also a great practical joker. WG had been playing in a festival match and all his appeals as a bowler had been turned down by the umpire, Farrands. At dinner that night, WG received a letter apparently written by the umpire, how he'd been hurt at the way WG had received his decisions. The Great Man retired to the smoking room to write a reply to the umpire, until he was told that it was O'Brien who had written the letter.

O'Brien headed the Middlesex batting averages for three consecutive seasons. His figures are worth recording:

	Inns	*NO*	*HS*	*Runs*	*Average*
1894	14	3	110	384	34.10
1895	25	3	202	833	40.30
1896	24	1	137	952	41.90

His highest innings for Middlesex was 202, made against Sussex at Hove, when he and Bob Lucas put on 338 in 200 minutes.

Even after his last game for Middlesex in 1898, he continued to play and in 1906, he hit 216 not out for Wiseton against Arthur Jones's team. He also captained the Gentlemen of Ireland in England and made a brilliant 167 against Oxford University and even at the age of 52 in 1914, made a first-class century. It came at Attleborough in Norfolk, when he was playing for Lionel Robinson's XI against Oxford University. After scoring 90 in the first innings at No 6, he opened in the second and scored 111 in 200 minutes to save the match.

By this time, he had become Sir Timothy O'Brien, after succeeding to the baronetcy on the death of his uncle Patrick.

When he died at Ramsey on the Isle of Man in December 1948 at the age of 87, he was the oldest Test match cricketer in England.

PETER PARFITT

Born: 8 December 1936, Billingford
Played: 1956–1972

FIRST-CLASS MIDDLESEX RECORDS

Matches	*Innings*	*NO*	*Runs*	*HS*	*Ave*	*100s*
387	665	84	21304	200*	36.67	46

Runs	*Wkts*	*Ave*	*Best*	*5wI*	*Ct*
6424	231	27.81	6-45	4	452

TEST MATCHES: 37

At Billingford, a tiny village in central Norfolk, Peter grew up in an atmosphere of cricket. When his two brothers left King Edward VII School, his father. gave him the choice of staying on or transferring to Fakenham Grammar School. He opted for the latter and so being a day school Fakenham gave him the opportunity to play games on a wider basis than would have been possible at a boarding school and his passage from schoolboy to county cricket was meteoric.

His father insisted that he did not play for his local Billingford side, but with a team several miles from his home whose main claim to fame was that they had a matting covered concrete wicket. Coached on a true wicket of even bounce and pace, he learnt to play strokes with great confidence, and at 17 he gained his Norfolk cap while still at school.

In the English Public and Grammar Schools soccer team, he played at left-half, his football skills earning him appearances in the same position as an amateur in the Norwich City team.

His application to study as a PE teacher at Loughborough College was unsuccessful – his disappointment and possibly frustration made him refuse to apply to the alternative college of St John's at York. Instead, he wrote to Bill Edrich who was captaining Middlesex and asked for a trial for the county.

Right from the outset of his career, he was considered to be Middlesex's most exciting batting prospect for years though he was also an off-break bowler. He could possibly have become an all-rounder if Fred Titmus hadn't been in the side.

Straight from school into county cricket was a strain for him. He made his Middlesex debut in their match against Yorkshire; walking past a certain Fred Trueman, he was addressed with the words 'Good morning, I hear you can hook!' He played in 14 matches in that 1956 season, his top score being 80 against Nottinghamshire at Trent Bridge, where he also bowled eight consecutive overs of off-spin and took a wicket without conceding a run – after which, he was omitted from the side!

He finished the season in the 2nd XI, before leaving for two years National Service where he played as much sport as he did as a civilian. When on leave from the RAF in 1958, he was able to play in 11 Championship matches, his top score was 99 at Leicester.

In his reappearance season of 1959, he scored 1300 runs and was capped the following summer.

Parfitt was a superb fielder in any position in his early years, though as his career progressed he specialised in the slips, where his agility made him outstanding. One of the best catchers of a ball that the game has seen, he holds the Middlesex record for most catches in a season by a non-wicket-keeper, 46 in both 1960 and 1966. Playing for the MCC against the South African Universities at Pietermaritzburg in 1964-65, he took five catches in an innings.

In 1961, he scored 2007 runs at an average of 39.35, with eight centuries. He hit 105 and 101 not out in the match against Nottinghamshire at Trent Bridge and was voted the Young Cricketer of the Year.

In 1962, he scored 2121 runs and finished ninth in the national batting average. He scored 122 and 114 for Middlesex against the Pakistanis at Lord's and also hit three Test hundreds against the Pakistanis, 101 not out at Edgbaston, 119 at Headingley and 101 not out at Trent Bridge, This last innings was his third hundred in successive innings within a week against the tourists and his sixth in seven innings against Pakistan bowling! He ended the series with an average of 113.00 and not surprisingly was selected as one of Wisden's 'Five Cricketers of the Year.'

In the first Test of the 1962-63 tour of Australia and New Zealand, Parfitt was England's top scorer with 80. He was tried as a Test opener, though it wasn't a successful switch and because he wasn't scoring runs in this position, he was left out of the Test side. He returned to his normal position for the Auckland Test, where he hit his highest ever Test score, 131 not out. He represented England on 37 occasions, scoring 1882 runs for an average of 40.91.

Even though he only had a modest Test series against Australia in 1964 and suffered from injuries, he topped the 1000 run mark from the 16 championship games in which he played. It was during this season, that he hit his highest score for Middlesex, 200 not out against Nottinghamshire at Trent Bridge.

He took over the Middlesex captaincy from Fred Titmus towards the end of the 1968 season, when the side were plunging towards the foot of the table. The last four matches of the season were won to give optimism for the future. He had two more seasons of captaincy, though the Middlesex committee were unduly slow to confirm him in this position.

Parfitt was something of a slow starter as a batsman, though once settled, he could be unorthodox as he attacked the bowling. In 1969, he showed his love for the Nottinghamshire and Trent Bridge ground, scoring 119 in the Gillette Cup, as he and Featherstone added 112 for the fourth wicket to establish a Middlesex record for that competition. This was also the season that he picked up 6 for 45 in the match against Oxford University.

In 1970, his last year as captain before being replaced by Mike Brearley, he topped the Middlesex batting averages. Parfitt had been badly treated by the Middlesex committee, but as it turned out the move worked out well. He had an excellent season in 1971 and batted well the following summer which was his last for the county. In fact, he was chosen to play in three Test matches that season.

Another Norfolk born player to captain Middlesex, he had a mercurial career.

IAN PEEBLES

Born: 20 January 1908, Aberdeen
Died: 27 February 1980
Played: 1928–1948

FIRST-CLASS MIDDLESEX RECORDS

Matches	*Innings*	*NO*	*Runs*	*HS*	*Ave*	*100s*
165	222	70	1361	58	8.95	0

Runs	*Wkts*	*Ave*	*Best*	*5wI*	*Ct*
12122	610	19.87	8-24	40	120

TEST MATCHES: 13

Ian Alexander Ross Peebles learned his cricket skills at the Glasgow Academy and as a 13 year old boy was discovered by George Geary when Leicestershire visited Scotland and advised him to try his luck in London.

He hoped to make a name for himself in the cricket world and was engaged by Aubrey Faulkner at his School of Cricket. The great all-rounder and coach offered him a secretarial job there and then, recognising Peebles' possibilities. He also impressed Pelham Warner, so much so that when it proved difficult in raising a good enough side to represent the Gentlemen against the Players at the Oval in 1927, he was given a place. At the time, he was a 19 year old playing for Chiswick Park; he celebrated his call-up by bowling Surrey's Andrew Sandham, to claim his and the first wicket of the match. He played later in the season at the Folkestone and Scarborough Festivals, but without much success.

Plum Warner was so impressed with Peebles, that he engineered a place for him on the strong but not representative MCC team to South Africa in 1927-28. He went officially as secretary to the captain, but he impressed with his bowling and was chosen for the first four Tests – he didn't do anything of note in the Tests, but took 34 wickets on the South African mat in other games.

In his first season for Middlesex, 1928, he played little and took only 14 wickets at a cost of 28 runs apiece. His rise the following season was somewhat unexpected; he was consistently among the top six bowlers in the country and sent down nearly a thousand overs. He took 107 wickets in championship matches (123 in all matches) – this was the year when for the only time in history three amateurs took 100 wickets for the same county, the other two being R W V Robins and N E Haig.

In 1930, he was at Oxford University, where he took 70 wickets, 13 of them for 231 against Cambridge; it was a catastrophic defeat for Oxford and reputedly the chances missed off him went into double figures. He then took 7 for 120 playing for the Gentlemen against the Players, his victims including Hobbs, Leyland and Sutcliffe. He was then chosen for the fourth Test at Old Trafford, where he came up against Bradman who had hit 131254 and 334 in the first three Tests. On a slow but not vicious turner, Peebles had him missed at first slip by Hammond, but then caught at second by Duleepsinhji for 14. He played in the fifth and final Test at the Oval and took 6 for 204 off 71 overs – this was better than anyone else. He ended the season at the top of the Middlesex bowling averages with 44 wickets at a cost of only 10.90 runs each.

In 1930-31, he had success in South Africa; in the fourth Test at Johannesburg, he ended his first innings spell with 5 for 18 in 9.5 overs, including 3 wickets with his last five balls – his final analysis was 6 for 63, his best in Test cricket. During this tour, he put the scorers to task – the scorebook entry reading: I A R Peebles – absent bathing! He was also England's best bowler in 1931 against New Zealand.

His figures in his first three full seasons of first-class cricket are worth setting down and show that he was head and shoulders above the rest of the Middlesex attack.

	Overs	*M*	*Runs*	*Wkts*	*Ave*
1929	957.4	200	2424	123	19.70
1930	871.4	143	2453	133	18.44
1931	962	165	2574	139	18.51

Of the English slow bowlers, only Parker (Gloucestershire) Freeman (Kent) and Richard Tyldesley (Lancashire) were consistently above him.

By now, the long winter days of bowling at Aubrey Faulkner's School as a teenager, followed by all the overs bowled in his early 20s, caused a muscular weakness of the shoulder, the effect of which was to take the fizz out of his leg breaks. At the School, he had taught himself to bowl left-arm, occasionally to relieve the strain. With the googly now his chief weapon, he remained a bowler to be reckoned with right up to the Second World War.

In 1932, he played in only 16 matches, taking 72 wickets, including a hat-trick against Gloucestershire at Lord's. In 1933, he claimed 45 wickets at a cost of 22 runs each and in the close season, he toured North America with Sir Julien Cahn's team and took 70 wickets at only 6 runs apiece. He only played in odd matches in the mid thirties, but in 1938, he returned a little to his old self, taking 32 wickets at 17.18.

In 1939, he succeeded Robins as captain, bringing Middlesex in (for the fourth successive year) as Championship runners-up.

During the Second World War, he sustained the almost total loss of his right eye, in an air-raid. Although he played a few games after the war up to 1948, his career really finished in terms of its effectiveness in 1939.

After his cricketing days were over, he entered the wine trade and also became a notable journalist, being Cricket Correspondent of *The Times* and contributor to *The Observer, The Guardian* and *The Cricketer.* He enjoyed writing about the game and produced several books, his autobiography *Spinner's Yarn* being the best, which in 1977 won the Cricket Society's Literary Award.

In and around 1930 when England was richer in leg-spin and googly bowling than ever before, or since, Ian Peebles was rated the best bowler of all. He died on 27 February 1980.

JOHN PRICE

Born: 22 July 1937, Harrow
Played: 1961–1975

FIRST-CLASS MIDDLESEX RECORDS

Matches	*Innings*	*NO*	*Runs*	*HS*	*Ave*	*100s*
242	191	80	902	41*	8.13	0

Runs	*Wkts*	*Ave*	*Best*	*5wI*	*Ct*
16440	734	22.40	8-48	25	89

TEST MATCHES: 15

A quick bowler from the Wembley Club, John Price joined Middlesex in 1961, playing in five matches and taking 18 wickets.

He began to play for the county on a regular basis in 1963, impressing immediately. At 26 in 1963 he had come to the game late and unfortunately, as he started to play Alan Moss retired. It would have been interesting to see them bowl together. Price worked up a good pace from a long winding run, but he never exploited the Lord's strip to the full, especially early in the opposition's innings. Coming into the game late, seemed a handicap though by the end of his first full season he had been awarded his county cap and called up to play for England against India in the close season.

He played 10 times for England between 1963 and 1965 and then at the age of 34, was recalled to the side for a further four matches in 1971, against Pakistan and India and a final appearance in 1972 against Australia at Lord's.

John Price was a sturdy right-arm fast bowler, having a round the corner run of quite some length. On his tour of India in 1963-64, he adopted Pythagoras' theorem – walking back to his mark along the shorter hypotenuse and running in round the other two sides. It was an ingenious method and conserved his energy in that intense heat, in fact, it was a method he retained for the rest of his career. On that tour of India, he hit his highest Test score on his debut at the crease, 32 at Bombay in the second Test. The third Test at Calcutta saw Price produce his best figures at Test level, 5 for 73.

Price had a high powerful body action and he could generate some pace – in the main, he swung the ball away, but he could also produce the occasional break-back.

During 1965, he was dogged by injury and missed much of the season, but in 1966 he regained both fitness and form. It was his best season, as he took 94 wickets in the championship at 18.74 each. He produced the best figures of his career at Lord's when he took 8 for 48 in the match against Derbyshire.

In 1969, more burden was thrown on Price's shoulders when Australian Test player Alan Connolly failed to play to his full capabilities It was the season when he hit an unbeaten 53 for D H Robins XI against the West Indies at Eastbourne. Later in his career he opened the Lord's Taverners innings against Corfu and scored a magnificent hundred. In fact, if he'd worked harder with his left-handed batting (for he had the reach and the strokes) he could have been classed in the all-rounder status.

In 1970, he was back to more like his old self and finished the season with 77 wickets at 2350 topping the Middlesex bowling averages.

He began the 1971 season in such fine form that he was recalled to the England side after a six year absence. He took 6 for 34 against Surrey in the Gillette Cup, though he was much more successful for England in terms of figures, for at the end of the season, his 45 wickets in the County Championship cost him over 30 runs each.

In the 1971 Test match at Lord's against Pakistan, he dismissed Wasim Bari and Asif Masood with successive deliveries, but was denied the chance of a hat-trick when Perez Sajjad was declared 'absent ill'.

As a fielder, Price had a safe pair of hands in the outfield; his throw having great power and a flat trajectory, right over the top of the stumps.

In 1972, his benefit year, he continued to bowl with great hostility and consistent pace, yet this was to be the last season in which he played on a regular basis, though he did play on occasions until 1975.

When he reappeared in August 1973, he showed just how much he'd been missed when he took 26 wickets in eight championship appearances at a low cost, but he also brought the best out of a young Mike Selvey. In 1974, he turned in his best Sunday League figures, when he took 4 for 27 against Sussex at Hove. He ended that 1974 season at the top of the Middlesex bowling averages with 21 wickets at 21.47 each and a best of 6 for 54.

The following season in the Benson and Hedges semi-final against Warwickshire at Edgbaston, Middlesex's opponents only needed 6 to win off the last over with three wickets in hand. John Price bowled this last over, taking 2 wickets as Warwickshire finished 4 runs short, unfortunately, Middlesex were easily beaten by Leicestershire in the final.

His cricketing career was restricted by back injuries, though it is a testimony to all the hard work and fine quality of bowling that he produced.

Some 13 years after he'd played his last first-class game, he was hospitalised when a virus seriously affected his heart. It was discovered whilst he was in hospital that he bowled throughout his career with a valve missing from his heart, which had amazingly withstood his great exertions as a quick bowler.

FRED PRICE

Born: 25 April 1902, Westminster
Died: 13 January 1969
Played: 1926–1947

FIRST-CLASS MIDDLESEX RECORDS

Matches	*Innings*	*NO*	*Runs*	*HS*	*Ave*	*100s*
382	555	96	8300	111	18.08	3

Runs	*Wkts*	*Ave*	*Best*	*5wI*	*Ct*	*St*
–	–	–	–	–	626	301

TEST MATCHES: 1

Making his Middlesex debut in 1926, Fred Price succeeded Murrell behind the stumps, maintaining his high-standards throughout his career until 1947 and in addition, batting valuably.

In 1929-30, he toured abroad for the first time with Hon. F S Calthorpe's MCC team, when he was sent to the West Indies as a replacement for the Major R T Stanyforth who was injured.

In 1933, he hit his highest ever first-class score, 111 off the Worcestershire bowling at Dudley, as he and Patsy Hendren added 352 for the fifth wicket. The following season, he failed narrowly to score two centuries in the same match against Kent at Lords, scoring 92 and 107. It was his best season with the bat as he scored 1298 runs.

He was a skilled wicket-keeper, especially strong on the leg-side and in

Middlesex's match against the South Africans at Lord's in 1935, he claimed eight victims (3 caught, 5 stumped).

Prior to the start of the 1937 season, he had spent a couple of weeks coaching in Selfridge's store. It must have worked wonders for in the match against Yorkshire at Lord's, he took 7 catches in the Tyke's first innings. After the match, a lady approached Price offering her congratulations, 'I was so thrilled with your performance Mr Price, I nearly fell off the balcony', to which Price responded 'If you had madam, I would have caught you as well!

In the close season, 1937-38 he went to South America with Sir Theodore Brinckman's side – the summer before had been his best behind the stumps as he dismissed 91 batsmen (65 caught and 26 stumped). His batting had improved so much since his early days, that when he played against Australia at Headingley in his one and only Test match, he batted at number 7. He was during the main part of his career, a contemporary of Les Ames the Kent wicket-keeper batsman who made 47 appearances for England. His batting that season led Middlesex to open the batting with him in several matches, Price ending the season with 818 runs at an average of 21.50. In the match against Warwickshire at Lords in 1938 he took 6 catches in their first innings.

The county were so pleased with Price's progress as a wicket-keeper, that in 1934 they released Andy Wilson who moved on to Gloucestershire.

After the hostilities were over, Fred Price was told that his services were no longer required. However, there was a wicket-keeping crisis in the county, for Cecil Maxwell, who had played for Nottinghamshire and was signed before the war, had obviously lost his talents in the seven years that we were without first-class cricket. Maxwell played in four games, before being replaced by another amateur, Horace King. The wicketkeeping problem was solved when Fred Price's employers were contacted and they agreed to release him to resume his cricket career at the age of 44; even so he was perky and irrepressible!

From 1950 to 1967, he was a first-class umpire, creating a sensation when he no-balled Surrey and England bowler Tony Lock three times for throwing against V S Hazare's Indian touring team at the Oval.

Also that same season, he officiated in the Surrey v Yorkshire game at the Oval. The Yorkshire batsmen were subjected to continuous barracking from the Surrey crowd as they struggled to avoid defeat. Price lay on the ground at square-leg until the noise subsided. He explained afterwards that the catcalls the Yorkshire batsmen were receiving just as they were to play the ball was certainly not his idea of sportsmanship. Fred Price went on to stand in eight Tests before his death at the age of 66 on 13 January 1969.

In all first-class matches, he fell just three short of 1,000 dismissals, with 312 of his victims being stumped.

George Mann

Bill Edrich

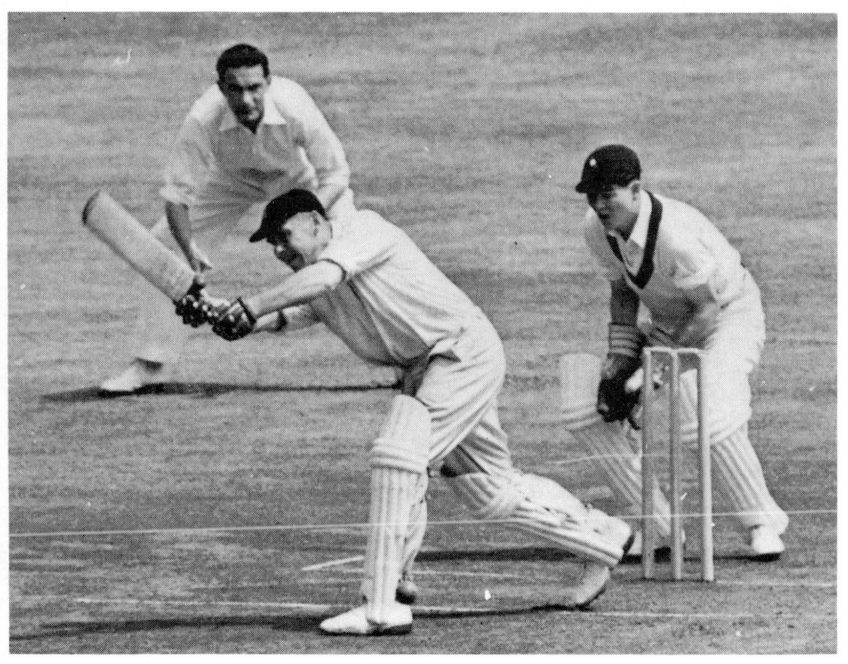
Syd Brown

Jack Robertson

John Warr

Freddie Titmus

Don Bennett

Alan Moss

Eric Russell

John Murray

Ron Hooker

Peter Parfitt

Bob Gale

Mike Smith

John Price

Mike Brearley

Clive Radley

Mike Selvey

Graham Barlow

Phil Edmonds

John Emburey

Roland Butcher

Mike Gatting

Wilf Slack

Wayne Daniel

Paul Downton

Norman Cowans

CLIVE RADLEY

Born: 13 May 1944, Hertford
Played: 1964–1987

FIRST-CLASS MIDDLESEX RECORDS

Matches	*Innings*	*NO*	*Runs*	*HS*	*Ave*	*100s*
512	813	132	24147	200	35.45	42

Runs	*Wkts*	*Ave*	*Best*	*5wI*	*Ct*
156	8	19.50	2-38	0	480

TEST MATCHES: 8

Born in Hertford, Clive Thornton Radley moved with his family to Norfolk and attended King Edward's Preparatory School. He failed his scholarship and entered King Edward VI Grammar School as a fee paying pupil. He played through the various teams until he was included in the 1st XI when he was still only fourteen. His father played for Norwich Wanderers, Clive following in his footsteps at the age of thirteen. Also that summer, he batted and bowled his leg breaks for Norfolk Schoolboys and in the year that he left King Edward's, he played under Bill Edrich in the Norfolk Minor Counties team.

Bill was still associated with Middlesex and it was he who suggested that they should take young Radley onto their staff. In the winter months, he returned home to Norfolk to play soccer for Yarmouth and had trials with Arsenal.

He made his county debut for Middlesex in 1964 against Lancashire at Old Trafford. He scored 21 before Geoff Clayton stumped him off the wily bowling of Sonny Ramadhin.

In 1965, only his second season, he helped Fred Titmus add 277 for the sixth wicket against the South Africans at Lord's – it is still the Middlesex record. Middlesex were in trouble at 72 for 5 when Titmus joined him. Radley's 138 was taken from an attack that contained Peter Pollock, Barlow and Dumbrill.

He played his first full season in 1967 when he was also awarded his county cap. His favourite drives and cuts were in evidence on the August Bank Holiday of that season, when he hit a glorious 19 off the Sussex attack. Also in 1967 he and Ron Hooker added 161 for the seventh wicket against Hampshire at Lord's.

In 1969, he was the only Middlesex batsman to exceed 1000 runs, finishing the season with an average of 40.61 (a lead of more than 10 on his next Middlesex colleague). He also hit an unbeaten 133 against Glamorgan at Lord's in the John Player League. He topped the Middlesex batting averages again in 1971 with 40.72. During the winter, he coached in South Africa for the Transvaal Cricket Union.

As a batsman, Clive Radley was most accomplished, a grafter of runs, with a fine temperament. His batting technique was based on sound defence. He took 480 first-class catches for Middlesex, the evidence of a superbly clean pair of hands, whether in the outfield, or in his preferred position at slip.

His unorthodox batting style and ability to improvise, put many a side in limited-overs games under great pressure. He scored centuries in all four competitions and hit hundreds off all the first-class counties.

By 1972, he was on the verge of international honours, after consistently scoring over 1000 runs in a season. In 1973, Radley was dismissed for 99 against Yorkshire at Lord's after putting 199 on with Brearley, who scored his first Championship hundred. He started the 1974 season with a bang, hitting a glorious century against Hampshire, proving throughout each season what a dependable player he was.

In 1975, he hit a marvellous 103 in the Benson and Hedges Semi-final against Warwickshire at Edgbaston. It was a season that saw him hit hundreds in other one-day competitions; 108 not out against Worcestershire in the Gillette Cup and 105 not out against Northamptonshire in the John Player League. Another unbeaten 121 followed in 1976 as Middlesex beat Minor Counties East at Lord's in the Benson and Hedges Cup. In the 1977 Gillette Cup Final against Glamorgan, he hit an unbeaten 85 to win the Man of the Match Award.

Clive was almost 34 when he was elevated from county to Test status. He made eight appearances for his country, not once being on the losing side. He scored 481 runs at an average of 48.10. His highest Test score was 158 made against New Zealand at Auckland. The innings lasted 648 minutes and was at the time, the longest innings in New Zealand. In 1978 he played in all the six Tests of the summer, hitting a further century, 108 against Pakistan.

In the Benson and Hedges Cup Final of 1983, Clive Radley once again won the Man of the Match Award with a commanding undefeated innings of 89 against Essex. It was an innings typical of Radley's cricket in his career at Middlesex. In the opening match of the 1984 County Championship campaign, he hit a quick-fire hundred against Glamorgan. In the Nat West Trophy Final this season, Middlesex beat Kent with Radley again named Man of the Match after an innings of 67, as Middlesex won off the last ball – it was the third time he'd scooped this award in a Lord's final.

In 1985, against Northamptonshire at Uxbridge, he hit the first double-century of his career – in his 41st year. He kept the score ticking over with his nudges and pushes. His score of 200 contained a six, a five and 26 fours, as he and Paul Downton added 289 for the fifth wicket. When Middlesex won the Championship this season and Radley topped the county's batting averages, Wisden remarked 'Radley enhanced his already high reputation for excavating runs from the deepest pit'.

In the Benson and Hedges final of 1986, he top scored for Middlesex with 54 as Kent failed by 2 runs to overtake Middlesex's score of 199 for 7.

Clive Radley had a benefit in 1977 and received a second one ten years later. Not many players have done more to earn the 'double'.

He was a magnificent team man and the most effective of batsmen. He played his last 1st XI game in 1987, but remains with the county, captaining the 2nd XI and is now MCC head coach. Few cricketers have given as much to the county of Middlesex or to the game of cricket itself.

JOHN RAWLIN

Born: 10 November 1856. Greasborough, Yorkshire
Died: 19 January 1924
Played: 1889–1909

FIRST-CLASS MIDDLESEX RECORDS

Matches	*Innings*	*NO*	*Runs*	*HS*	*Ave*	*100s*
229	358	31	5680	100	17.57	1

Runs	*Wkts*	*Ave*	*Best*	*5wI*	*Ct*
13277	659	20.15	8-29	34	159

TEST MATCHES: 0

Born in Greasborough near Rotherham, John Thomas Rawlin played for Yorkshire, his native county in 1880. He went on to play his last game for them in 1885, a grand total of five matches!

In 1887, he came south to qualify for Middlesex, becoming a member of the MCC ground-staff a position he maintained until 1911. In 1887-88, he visited Australia with Mr G F Vernon's team for his only overseas trip.

He probably hadn't got the nerve to show his face again in the village of his birth. Rawlin was one of the first bowlers to exploit a 'swerve' – as in those days they called the flight of a ball which swayed in the air this way or that. A fast-medium bowler with a high delivery action, his ability to make the ball break both ways was his trademark. He was also a hard-hitting batsman, who once set, could score quite freely.

He made his Middlesex debut in 1889 and two years later gave Hearne fine support with 65 championship wickets at a cost of 12.50 runs each, as Middlesex ended the season in third place. In this season of 1891, he both batted and bowled with considerable success and along with Hearne, he was responsible for skittling out Surrey for 119 to win the game, after Middlesex followed on 179 behind. His best figures that season were his 8 for 64 against Somerset at Taunton, though when playing for the MCC against Nottinghamshire at Lord's he had a bowling analysis of 4 for 8.

In 1892, he took 78 championship wickets at a slightly higher cost of 17 runs each. He bowled unchanged with J T Hearne against Sussex at Hove though he reserved his best figures of the season, 8 for 54 for his native county Yorkshire at Headingley.

In 1893, he had his best season for Middlesex, taking 90 championship wickets at 14 runs apiece, though he took 104 in all matches. During this summer, Gloucestershire were skittled out for 72 and 47 with John Rawlin having match figures of 12 for 60, including 8 for 29 in the match at Bristol. The following year, he took 8 for 50 against the county of his birth at Sheffield.

As a bowler, Rawlin's last season of note was really 1895 when his figures included a great performance of 7 for 18 against Nottinghamshire at Lord's. After this, he concentrated on his batting a little more, this enabling him to play right up to 1909 when he was 52 years old.

In 1896, he was awarded the first of two benefits against Somerset, the second came some fifteen years later against Sussex. In his first benefit match against Somerset, he got a duck and failed to take a wicket as Middlesex won by an innings. Against Surrey that season, Rawlin and Hearne bowled unchanged; Rawlin taking 4 for 15 and 4 for 54. He ended the season with 52 wickets at a cost of over 25 runs each, which was fairly expensive by current standards – he was now 40 years of age.

In 1899, at the age of 42, he hit his highest first-class score exactly 100 against near rivals Surrey; he was now in his later years a painstaking batsman.

In 1901, he took only 23 championship wickets, his best being 5 for 88 in the drawn encounter with Surrey at the Oval.

Rawlin also appeared for the Players against the Gentlemen in 1892, 1895 and 1896.

After taking 659 first-class wickets for Middlesex, he retired in 1909, dying fifteen years later in his native place on 19 January at the age of 66.

JACK ROBERTSON

Born: 22 February 1917, Chiswick
Played: 1937–1959

FIRST-CLASS MIDDLESEX RECORDS

Matches	*Innings*	*NO*	*Runs*	*HS*	*Ave*	*100s*
423	745	39	27088	331*	38.37	59

Runs	*Wkts*	*Ave*	*Best*	*5wI*	*Ct*
2006	56	35.82	4-37	0	301

TEST MATCHES: 11

Coming from Chiswick in West London, he was coached by Jack Durston at the Acton Cricket School and used to open Turnham Green's batting with his father.

He made his Middlesex debut in the rain-ruined match against Oxford University at The Parks in 1937, batting at No 6 and scoring 0. It was his only match that summer, but after being offered a contract for the 1938 season he began to establish himself as the third leading run-getter behind Edrich and Compton. He came into the side in that 1938 season for the Whitsun match with Sussex at Lord's in early June. He scored a masterly 81, as he and Edrich added 129 for the first wicket. In 1939, he scored 1755 runs at an average of 40 with four centuries to his name. One of these came in the last great burst of scoring prior to the war, when Middlesex scored 525 for 7 declared, beating Warwickshire by an innings inside two days.

In those two pre-war seasons, he impressed all those who saw him by the power and timing of his batting.

During the later stages of the war, Jack Robertson was stationed with the Army at Bovington Camp in Dorset, where he had no facility for practice. At intervals, he was summoned to Lord's to represent England against the Australian Services – he had to get his practice in the middle and averaged 34 in the Victory Series.

In 1944, during a game between the Army and the RAF, the descent of a flying bomb caused the players to fling themselves flat on the turf; after they had all picked themselves up, the next ball was hooked famously for six by Captain J D B Robertson.

He returned to Middlesex after the war, aged 29, to play absolutely brilliantly, not seeming to have missed those important years.

He started and finished the 1946 season in fine form, but was a little indifferent in between. Nevertheless he scored more runs for Middlesex than anyone else, hitting 5 centuries and averaging 42. On a drying pitch, he hit 104 of Middlesex's total of 242 against Kent, helping to lay to rest the theory that he couldn't play leg-spin bowling he took Doug Wright to pieces – he followed this next season with 110 from Middlesex's total of 229 against the same opposition.

Robertson possessed an elegant array of off-side strokes and produced straight drives hit with immense power.

In 1947, his opening partnerships with Syd Brown were invaluable in preparing the way for Edrich and Compton to display their talents. Against Nottinghamshire at Lord's, he and Brown added 310 for the first wicket – a new record, though since twice beaten. His innings of 183 contained 3 sixes, a five and 14 fours. Against Hampshire, he hit the first double century of his career, 229 in five hours, as Middlesex won by an innings. He played in one Test against the South Africans and played in the Gentlemen v Players match at Lord's. In Championship matches that season, he scored 2214 runs at an average of 65 and beat all but four other county batsmen in England. His total in all matches was 2760 (Average 52.00) and included 12 centuries.

His first overseas tour was to the West Indies in 1947-48 when he was the leading Test batsman with an average of 55, having totalled more than 100 runs in each of the first two Tests.

He wasn't far from reaching 1000 runs in May 1948. He was in such fine form at the beginning of that season, with 66 and 154 for the MCC v Surrey and 75 and 74 for Middlesex v Hampshire and later 147 and 137 against Sussex, that by mid-May, he had totalled close on 700 runs. He was however, unable to keep up the pace in the last two weeks and ended with a total of just 800.

In that match at Lord's when representing the MCC in their match against Surrey, he scored 9 runs off one ball from H S Squires, it included of course four runs for overthrows.

He ended the season with 2366 runs in all matches for an average of 50 – a magnificent performance when he had to 'carry the side' in the absence of both Compton and Edrich who were on Test match duty. As a batsman, he had the economy of movement and an impeccable style – a firm driver of the ball, he was a quick scorer when he was in the mood.

Just how difficult it was for Jack Robertson to make the Test team was well illustrated by the events of 1949. He replaced Lancashire's Cyril Washbrook who was injured, in the second Test against New Zealand at Lord's. After scoring 26 in the first innings, he scored 121 in the second, having shared an opening stand of 143. It seemed that he had seized his chance, but he was dropped for the next Test! On the very day that the third Test started, Jack Robertson produced his most majestic cricket. In six and a half hours, he hit two sixes and 39 fours in an unbeaten innings of 331 against Worcestershire. It remains the highest score for the county and the feat of scoring over 300 runs in a day wasn't repeated until 1982, when Glenn Turner did so on the same ground. It was also a season when Robertson and Brown shared their most significant opening partnerships against the two northern counties – 207 against Lancashire (Robertson 159) and 198 against Yorkshire (Robertson 113).

Against Hampshire at Portsmouth in 1951, he scored 135 as he and Syd Brown added 232 in not more than three hours. In championship matches alone, he scored 2542 runs–2917 in all games. This was his benefit year and he couldn't have been in better form. Against Somerset he hit 75 in the first innings and then when he made 201 not out in the second, he became the first batsman in the country to pass 2000.

For the seventh successive season in 1952, he reached over 2000 runs in all matches – a magnificent record, unapproached by any other county player in the land.

He began the 1953 season in great form and early on, made hundreds in three successive matches, but was then put out of the game with a groin injury.

During the period 1954-58, he was holding his form much more than Compton or Edrich and topped the 1000 run mark in each season. In County Championship matches his record was:

1954	1292	at 29.36
1955	1754	at 31.89
1956	1386	at 29.48
1957	1852	at 37.79
1958	1467	at 34.93

In 1957, he scored 2028 runs in all matches and hit his last double hundred, 201 not out against Essex at Lord's. In 1958 his top score was 99 in the second half of the season, and he was used to bolster the middle order. His form deserted him in 1959, his second Benefit year, when he could only score 326 for an average of under 15.

Jack Robertson, a superb opening batsman, should have represented his country more times than he did.

On his retirement from the first-class game, he became Middlesex coach and spent much of his spare time lecturing young cricketers. He even continued to open the batting for the Lord's Taverners until he was well into his sixties.

WALTER ROBINS

Born: 3 June 1906, Stafford
Died: 12 December 1968
Played: 1925–1951

FIRST-CLASS MIDDLESEX RECORDS

Matches	*Innings*	*NO*	*Runs*	*HS*	*Ave*	*100s*
258	378	24	9337	140	26.38	6

Runs	*Wkts*	*Ave*	*Best*	*5wI*	*Ct*
14907	669	22.28	8-69	38	142

TEST MATCHES: 19

Walter Robins was taught the rudiments of the game by his father, a Staffordshire cricketer and from an early age, he assisted his local East Molesey Cricket Club.

He was one of the most talented schoolboy cricketers at Highgate, where in three of his four years there he headed both the batting and bowling averages. In 1925, he was captain; it was a tremendous last season for him, as he scored 816 runs at an average of 62.76 and took 60 wickets at a cost of 15.18 runs apiece. His best performance came in the schools match against Aldenham, when he hit a masterly 206 and took 7 for 54.

He had been to Lord's in 1924 as a schoolboy, making 97 and 0 for The Rest against the Lord's Schools and then opened the innings for the Public Schools against the Army and was dismissed for 1 and 0.

He was also captain of the Highgate 1st XI soccer team and made his Middlesex debut in 1925.

As a Cambridge Freshman in 1926, he obtained his Blue purely as a batsman, scoring 37 and 21 not out. He hit 55 and 41 in the Varsity Match of 1927, but in 1928, he not only scored 53 and 101 not out, but had match figures of 8 for 151, almost bringing victory to the Cambridge side. That performance brought him the first of many appearances in the Gentlemen's team against the Players.

Also whilst at Cambridge, he played on the right-wing in the University matches of 1926, 1927 and 1928, as well as representing the Corinthians and Notts Forest.

In his first full season for Middlesex in 1929, he achieved his only 'double' scoring 1134 runs (Average 26.37), including one century and taking 162 wickets (Average 21.53) but more than once he came near to repeating the feat. Twice he did the hat-trick for Middlesex, against Leicestershire that summer and then eight years later against Somerset, both at Lord's. His best figures were 8 for 69 against Gloucestershire – his season's haul, the reward of leg-spin and 'googlies', were taken despite Ian Peebles, also leg-spinning and 'googling' for Middlesex in the same season taking 107 wickets at 19.43. Amongst the wickets which fell to young Robins in 1929 were those of Hammond, Hobbs, Hallows, George Gunn, Ernest Tyldesley and Les Ames – all top-class England batsman.

In 1930, he bowled Bradman at Trent Bridge in his first English Test, the famous batsman not offering a stroke – this leading to England's only victory that summer. It wasn't too long after this, that he was persuaded to slow down and give the ball more air.

As a bowler, his action of a hopping cock-sparrow like run was a familiar sight at Lord's. He would give the ball a heavy finger twist and then go on a jinking follow-up down the wicket. He probably bowled (not all good!) a greater variety of balls than any other bowler of his day. His repertoire included googlies, leg-breaks and top-spinner, mixed in with the ball that cut in from the off to cause pandemonium. He was the sort of leg-spinner that could win and nearly lose a match in half-an-hour.

He took over the leadership of Middlesex in 1935, when the county side had shown some inexplicably bad form. Within his first season, he had changed all this and the county finished third in the championship. He Inspired his players to go all out for victory, leading by example. He added both an audacity and originality to his own aggressive play, and his knowledge of the game equalled his skill and appetite for cricket. Middlesex remained in second place for the next three seasons.

In 1937, Robins was so exhilarated by his sides close run against Yorkshire for the title, that he threw down a challenge to Brian Sellars to play a deciding charity match and the Yorkshire captain accepted. The game was played at the Oval in mid-September. To be fair, Middlesex didn't have the best of the conditions and Yorkshire won by an innings and 115 runs!

He played in 19 Tests for his country, being captain for the 1937 home series against New Zealand. His highest score in Test cricket was 108 against South Africa at Old Trafford in 1935, at a time when runs were sorely needed. His best bowling at Test level was 6 for 32 against the West Indies at Lord's in 1933. His one major tour abroad was to Australia in 1936-37 as vice-captain under Gubby Allen. Unfortunately for Robins, he broke a finger on his right hand during fielding practice in the first week of the tour, with the result that he couldn't spin the ball as much and thus limited his bowling successes.

In his last Test in 1937 against New Zealand at the Oval, he ended their first innings with a 7-ball spell of 3 for 1!

When cricket resumed after the war, he led them to second place and then in 1947, like Plum Warner some twenty seven years before him, he led them to the championship in his last year as captain. It is highly probable to say, that if he had been able to play regularly and lead the side, Middlesex must have won again in 1948.

As a batsman, he made the most use of his feet, often going out of his crease to the shortest of deliveries and taking the ball high up on his bat. His best shots were the cover-drive and a lofted straight hit past the bowler. In 1948, he hit 101 in 91 minutes against Kent at Dover.

Walter Robins was very interested in the history and scientific side of bowling. It was felt by Arthur Mailey that if he'd been more interested in attaining a great amount of wickets, he'd have been more effective.

As a Test selector, he served from 1946-49 and then again in 1954. In 1951, at the age of 45, he captained the MCC team which visited Canada, meeting with considerable success.

He was Chairman of the Test selection committee from 1962 to 1964 and was also manager of the MCC team in the West Indies in 1959–60.

He died at his home near Lord's on 12 December 1968, one of the most dynamic of all-round cricketers of his time.

ERIC RUSSELL

Born: 3 July 1936, Dumbarton
Played: 1956–1972

FIRST-CLASS MIDDLESEX RECORDS

Matches	*Innings*	*NO*	*Runs*	*HS*	*Ave*	*100s*
400	712	54	23103	193	35.11	37

Runs	*Wkts*	*Ave*	*Best*	*5wI*	*Ct*
643	10	64.30	2-46	0	274

TEST MATCHES: 10

Eric Russell comes from Dumbarton in Scotland, where his father ran his own clothing business in Glasgow, but when he was still very young, the family moved south to Harrow and he wasn't long in joining Atholl House, a small private school in Pinner.

It was here that his natural ability as a ball player gained him a place in both the soccer and cricket teams. However, his real development in terms of cricket, came when at the age of 13, he played for the Harrow Town 3rd XI. Such was his progress, that when he left school at 15, he was recommended to the Lord's ground-staff, starting work there straightaway.

By the time he had reached 19, he was offered a contract by Middlesex and made his first-team debut in July 1956 against Kent. It was a difficult baptism as Doug Wright was baffling all the batsmen and young Russell had yet to develop a technique for playing such bowling – he like many other good players started with a duck.

After playing in only one championship match the following summer, he had made the opening position his own by the middle of 1958. In the match against Leicestershire, he and Bob Gale began the first of many fruitful stands. They put on 96 and 113 for the first wicket in each innings, with Russell's contributions being 40 and 46.

Yet during his early years at Lord's he was regarded as something of an all-rounder, batting in the middle-order and bowling leg-breaks. He was a batsman of the utmost elegance; his hitting on the offside off either foot and his leg-glancing delighted spectators throughout his career. Though he only took 10 first-class wickets for Middlesex, his philosophy on bowling wouldn't I'm sure be appreciated by recognised bowlers. 'There's not much in bowling really, just direction and length and let the pitch do the rest.'

In 1960, in all matches, he fell just short of 2000 runs and was selected for the Players side at Lord's, where he scored 55 not out and 39.

His best year was 1964, when he scored 2342 runs at an average of 45.92 with five centuries. His highest score of 193 was made against Hampshire, yet this was perhaps not as great an innings as his 158 against Lancashire when he held the Middlesex side together while wickets tumbled around him to the superb bowling of Brian Statham. It was the first time since the early post-war years a Middlesex batsman exceeded 2000 runs in championship matches alone.

At the end of the 1965 season, he was chosen to tour Australia and New Zealand. He played in only the first Test and this was marred by splitting the webbing between the third and fourth finger of his right hand while fielding, thereby causing him to bat at number 11, giving Geoff Boycott the opportunity to establish himself as an England opener. He had started the tour so well, with scores of 42, 93, 0 not out until the Queensland game where he had made a chanceless 110 until stumped by Wally Grout. In the second innings, he had reached 45 when fast bowler Peter Allan hit him on the right thumb causing a hair-line fracture. A philosophical man, Russell accepted these incidents and the loss of his Test place, finishing the tour fourth in the batting averages with 58. On the New Zealand leg of the tour, he took 3 for 20 against the President's XI, bowling off-spin not his usual leg breaks.

In 1967, he was the first batsman to reach 1000 runs. Against the Pakistanis, he and Mike Harris scored 312 for the first wicket; his century helping him win back his Test place. His last innings in Test cricket saw him score 43 before he was bowled by Intikhab Alam. He represented England on 10 occasions, scoring 362 runs with a top score of 70 against South Africa at the Oval in 1965.

In his early days, he was exciting in the outfield, but later developed into a fine close to the wicket catcher.

In his benefit year of 1969, he batted well in the early part of the season, but then his batting went to pieces, possibly with the anxiety associated with such time.

It wasn't too long before his confidence returned, for in 1970, he and Mike Smith put on 131 and 140 in unfinished partnerships against Oxford University, and then in 1971, he exceeded 1500 runs. He left Middlesex at the end of the 1972 season and had two additional seasons with Berkshire.

Meticulous in his dress, his batting simply mirrored that. For sixteen seasons, he was among the most stylish and accomplished of county openers – his 23103 runs, an acknowledgement of his success.

MIKE SELVEY

Born: 25 April 1948, Chiswick
Played: 1972–1982

FIRST-CLASS MIDDLESEX RECORDS

Matches	*Innings*	*NO*	*Runs*	*HS*	*Ave*	*100s*
210	212	65	1835	67	12.48	0

Runs	*Wkts*	*Ave*	*Best*	*5wI*	*Ct*
15653	615	25.45	7-20	33	56

TEST MATCHES: 3

Mike Selvey played his cricket at Battersea Grammar School, Beddington Cricket Club, Surrey and the Universities of Manchester and Cambridge before he joined Middlesex at the age of 24.

He made his Surrey debut in 1968 at the age of 20. A strongly built, tall bowler who could swing the ball both ways, his high action often resulted in an alarming bounce. He played both soccer and cricket for Cambridge winning his Blue in 1971.

Selvey made his Middlesex debut in 1972, impressing with his stamina and his ability to move the ball. Initially, he seemed quite quick, but he didn't maintain his pace, though he certainly gained in control and was more than willing to bowl in long spells. He took 6 for 43 in the championship match against Sussex and also produced his best ever figures in the Benson and Hedges Cup match against Gloucestershire, taking 5 for 39 from his 11 overs.

In the last match of the 1973 season at Bradford against Yorkshire, the white-rose county required 208 to win. The scores were tied with Yorkshire on 207 for 9 when Selvey removed Robinson's middle stump. It was the season in which Mike Selvey was deservedly awarded his county cap. During the close season, he went to play for the Orange Free State in South Africa.

The 1974 season was a disappointing one for Selvey. It began well, as he took 9 wickets in the opening match against Hampshire, but he lost his form and his place as the season progressed. By the following season, he had recovered his lost zest and control, taking 64 wickets with a best of 6 for 59; he also produced his best Sunday League figures, taking 5 for 18 against Glamorgan.

Mike Selvey was in outstanding form in 1976; he took 11 wickets in the match against Oxford University and 6 against Kent at Lord's in the first match in the County Championship. Opening the bowling with Allan Jones (ex Sussex and Somerset), Selvey was helped in the destruction of Essex, Somerset and Gloucestershire. It was against Gloucestershire that Selvey produced his best first-class figures, 7 for 20 as the West Country side were dismissed for 55. It was after this performance, that he was included in the England side after a spate of injuries had robbed them of their regular bowling attack.

He was called up for the third Test against the West Indies at Old Trafford, in a match I remember well. He dismissed Roy Fredericks with his sixth ball and took 3 for 6 in his first 20 balls, including Clive Lloyd, the West Indian captain. He finished the innings with 4 for 41 from 17 overs.

Selvey had another good season in 1977, taking 78 wickets at 19.74 each. In the Gillette Cup Final that season against Glamorgan, he bowled his spell to great effect to finish with the following figures:

0	*M*	*R*	*W*
12	4	22	2

His victims being Alan Jones and West Indian Collis King.

In 1978, Mike Selvey was one of only four bowlers to take over a hundred wickets. Allied to his usual stamina, he had added more aggression. Coupled with his ability to move the ball about so much, made him trouble all the top batsmen in the country. During the last few weeks of the County Championship it was Selvey's form that was the driving force behind Middlesex's winning of eight of their last ten games to end the season in third place in the Championship. Selvey's 101 first-class wickets costing 19.09 runs each.

In the Gillette Cup Final of 1980, Selvey again bowled extremely well to help dismiss Surrey for 201. His figures were.

O	*M*	*R*	*W*
12	5	17	2

His victims being Alan Butcher and Graham Clinton. The following season, he was one of 11 Middlesex international players on duty for the match against Essex.

He left Middlesex at the end of the 1982 season to play for Glamorgan, but a persistent knee injury ended his career after two seasons. He now imparts his knowledge of the game to many avid readers of his column as cricket correspondent of *The Guardian*.

Selvey's contribution to Middlesex cannot be measured by his figures alone. He was an enthusiastic and energetic team man who bowled tirelessly for his county at times when others didn't want to know.

JIM SIMS

Born: 13 May 1903
Died: 27 April 1973
Played: 1929–1952

FIRST-CLASS MIDDLESEX RECORDS

Matches	*Innings*	*NO*	*Runs*	*HS*	*Ave*	*100s*
381	515	96	7173	121	17.12	3

Runs	*Wkts*	*Ave*	*Best*	*5wI*	*Ct*
31708	1257	25.23	9-92	77	202

TEST MATCHES: 4

Making his Middlesex debut in 1929, James Morton Sims was considered mainly as a batsman, and regularly opened the innings. He developed into an all-rounder and particularly after the Second World War was relied upon mainly for his bowling. In 1931, he hit a century in an MCC match against Kent, thus earning him a second trial with the county, after being unlucky at first. His bowling at this time was rather erratic and expensive and his batting unimaginative. If the Middlesex XI had not been so up and down, he wouldn't have lasted the pace.

Jim Sims was quite devastating on his day with his leg-break and googly. In 1933 he dismissed three Derbyshire batsmen in the course of four balls at Chesterfield. He used to revel on a dry, dusty track, because he bowled his leg-break so quickly. At Old Trafford in 1934, he demolished the Lancashire batting, taking 9 for 92. His first hundred for Middlesex was in 1932, but in the 1934 season against Surrey at the Oval, his innings of 103 as he opened the batting, took him 280 minutes. He ended the season with 639 runs for an average of just over 20.

He toured Australasia under E R T Holmes in 1935-36 and under Gubby Allen the following winter. In the latter of these tours, he did well in the state matches, but in the two Tests he was called upon to play, he proved quite costly on the hard pitches.

He played in two other Tests for England, against South Africa in 1935 and against India in 1936, both at home. His best figures with the ball were 5 for 73 at the Oval in the 1936 match with India.

Sims dismissed over 100 batsmen in a season on eight occasions, his best being 1939, when he took 143 championship wickets at 20.55 runs each. He was also a match-winner, averaging 38 balls a wicket – as it was a year that they experimented with eight-ball overs, he managed to take a wicket every fifth over. He had fourteen 5 wicket hauls and took 8 for 32 as Derbyshire were bowled out for 110 and another five wickets in the second. He was bowling so well in this last season before the war, that he must have had an excellent chance of making a second tour to Australia in 1940. In fact, the six years of hostilities put an end to Sims Test prospects.

He was certainly one of cricket's greatest characters; famous for his wit and dead-pan asides delivered from the side of his mouth and behind his hand. Jim Sims was also a great leg-puller and teller of cricketing anecdotes.

His classic was his reply to his skipper's reprimand at Trent Bridge. His batting against Harold Larwood left much to be desired. When finally his middle stump was uprooted, Jim was near enough to the square leg umpire. On returning to the dressing room, he was confronted by Walter Robins who said rather sharply, 'Jim that was a poor effort – you were frightened and worse still you made no attempt to hide it. ' 'Not exactly frightened Mr Robins came the reply, Shall we say just a little apprehensive and leave it at that!'

On another occasion, he dismissed a very capable batsman with a googly, remarking to the nearest fieldsman; I'd been keeping that one warm all through the winter. It was also Jim who suffered what is the bowler's nightmare, three successive balls that shaved the lucky batsman's stumps, a fate which would have probably driven the average bowler to profanity. Jim turned to his captain with a winning smile, 'Remarkable, Mr Robins' he murmured equably and just as equably completed the over.

In 1947, even though he was kept out of the game for a number of weeks by a broken finger, he took 100 wickets. At Lord's that summer, he performed the hat-trick against Alan Melville's South African team.

In 1948, playing against one of his favourite opposing sides, Surrey, he bowled his side to an innings victory, taking 7 for 58 and for 64. He also had a good match against the Australians that season, taking 6 for 65, though Middlesex were beaten by ten wickets.

He was going to retire at the end of the 1948 season, but after taking all ten wickets in the Kingston Festival match, he stayed on for another four seasons '

After retiring, he had charge of the county 2nd XI and served as coach until taking over the post of scorer. His appointment as deputy head coach was at a time when a great deal was being done to restructure Middlesex and put it on a more professional basis.

He had been scorer for a number of years, his death occurring while he was staying at a Canterbury hotel on the night preceding a pre-season game with Kent.

In all first-class matches, he took 1582 wickets – a great achievement for a rare and endearing character.

WILF SLACK

Born: 12 December 1954, Troumaca, West Indies
Died: 15 January 1989
Played: 1977–1988

FIRST-CLASS MIDDLESEX RECORDS

Matches	*Innings*	*NO*	*Runs*	*HS*	*Ave*	*100s*
201	348	38	12565	248*	40.53	25

Runs	*Wkts*	*Ave*	*Best*	*5wI*	*Ct*
632	19	33.26	3-17	0	139

TEST MATCHES: 3

Migrating from the Windward Islands to High Wycombe with his Parents when he was 11 years old, Wilf Slack played his early cricket for his town club.

In 1972, he played for the village of Frieth in the Village Championship and in 1976, was chosen to represent Buckinghamshire, where he was spotted by the Middlesex coach, Don Bennett.

He joined Middlesex in 1977 and for the first few seasons, was feeling his way. He certainly didn't seem to like opening the batting, yet this was to be the position he occupied once he had cemented his first team place.

As an opening batsman, he had a succession of partners – Brearley, Downton, Barlow (the most successful of all), Miller, Brown and Carr. He made the greatest advance of all Middlesex batsmen in 1981. His chance came to open the innings with Graham Barlow, as Brearley was away on Test duty, and wicket-keeper Downton had moved down the order.

Wilf Slack was a left-handed batsman and a very sound player of fast bowling, being primarily a front-foot player. He had immense concentration – during a morning session, he would often play and miss, whilst other batsmen looked more secure, but it was Wilf who was still there when lunchtime arrived. His dealings with the short-pitched delivery were admired by his colleagues – his technique probably the result of three seasons Shell Shield cricket whilst playing for the Windward Islands from 1981–83.

At Lord's in mid-July 1981, in the match against Kent, Slack and Barlow shared an unbeaten stand of 367 for the first wicket in the county's second innings – a new Middlesex record, and one that is likely to stand for a long time, if not forever. Slack's innings of 181 contained three sixes and 20 fours.

Later that summer, Wilf Slack hit the highest score of his career, 248 not out against Worcestershire. This was after Hartley Alleyne had shot the county out or 120 in their irst innings.

He was now batting with great resolution and in 1982 scored an unbeaten 203 against Oxford University at The Parks.

For three years between 1983-85, Slack and Barlow were probably the best opening combination in the country. Wilf Slack was also a very handy right-arm medium-pace change bowler and an agile fielder who usually fielded at short-leg. But, it was as an opening batsman that Slack shone, becoming increasingly solid and most productive.

In 1985, he carried his bat for 72 against Worcestershire at Lords in a Middlesex total of 195. However, it was his innings of 201 not out against the Australians that put him in the limelight.

He was selected to tour Sri Lanka with the England 'B' side in 1985-86. It was after a successful run with the 'B' team that he was drafted into the full England party who were touring the West Indies. Despite seeing England off to a good start with a solid 52 in the Antigua Test, he was only to score 81 runs at an average of 13.50 in the three Tests he played against the West Indies and India in 1986. He played in only two One-Day Internationals, both against the West Indies, scoring 33 and 10.

In 1986, he set a new Middlesex first wicket record in the John Player League, as he and A Miller put on 148 against Yorkshire at Lord's; Slack's score being 101 not out. He also carried his bat for 105 not out from Middlesex's score of 252 against Yorkshire at Headingley in a County Championship match.

He was a member of the England touring party to Australia in 1986-87, but spent much of the tour confined to the sidelines. Soon afterwards, he passed out in Tasmania, the first of a series of fainting fits. He was one of the fittest players on the county circuit, but in 1988, he suffered three further mysterious black-outs. Two of them were at the wicket and one whilst he was fielding. He had extensive tests to try and get to the root of the cause, but no one seemed to have diagnosed the problem properly, for he was passed fit to play.

He had a successful season in 1988, hitting 1228 runs at 45.48 in all first-class matches and hitting 163 not out and 105 not out against Glamorgan at Lord's,

It was the saddest news of England's tourless winter of 1988-89 to learn of Wilf Slack's death at the age of 34, on a private tour of The Gambia on 15 January 1989.

JIM SMITH

Born: 25 August 1906, Corsham, Wiltshire
Died: 9 February 1979
Played: 1934–1939

FIRST-CLASS MIDDLESEX RECORDS

Matches	*Innings*	*NO*	*Runs*	*HS*	*Ave*	*100s*
152	216	23	2977	101*	15.42	1

Runs	*Wkts*	*Ave*	*Best*	*5wI*	*Ct*
12001	676	17.75	8-102	39	69

TEST MATCHES: 5

Cedric Ivan James Smith, better known as 'Big Jim' was born at Corsham, near Chippenham in Wiltshire. He and his brother Walter had opened the bowling for Wiltshire in Minor county cricket for many years before Jim was taken on the groundstaff at Lord's. He was heralded as a 'new Jessop', though an administrative slip-up led to him having to qualify for five years, playing for the MCC before he could play for Middlesex.

He was almost 28 years old when he made his debut for Middlesex in 1934. 'Big Jim' Smith was at 6ft 4ins, a tall and immensely strong right-arm fast bowler; his first season turned him into something of a cricketing legend. Opening the bowling he took 172 wickets at a cost of 18.88 runs each and finished sixth in the national bowling averages. He also represented the Players against the Gentlemen at Lord's and was chosen by Wisden as one of their Five Cricketers of the Year.

He was only able to play for the county for six seasons before the war interrupted and ended his career. During that time, he took 676 first-class wickets for Middlesex, yet it is as Smith the batsman that he is best remembered.

Some of his most sensational hitting came on the MCC tour of the West Indies in 1934-35, when he shared in a last wicket stand of 122 in 45 minutes with Wally Hammond. Smith's contribution was 83 (five sixes and 9 fours); Hammond went on to 281 not out. In the third Test at Georgetown, he was promoted up the order after the openers had scored 38 in one and a half hours; he hit three sixes and scored 25 in ten minutes. In his first Test match in Barbados on that tour, he bagged a pair as rain fell rapidly on an already rain-affected wicket.

In his heyday, he weighed seventeen and a half stone, though he reached nineteen stone on his return from the West Indies. He wore size fourteen boots which he had specially made to order every year.

In 1935, he hit 53 in 41 minutes against Derbyshire – the first of his power shows of hitting. Later that season at Maidstone, he hit a fifty in 14 minutes, he also played in a charity match at Rayner's Lane; going in at

No 9 against XV of Harrow and District, he hit 173 in seven minutes short of an hour! His innings consisted of 19 sixes and 12 fours – eight balls being lost, otherwise his rate of scoring would have been faster!

As a bowler, Smith wasn't particularly fast, but his accuracy, great height and ability to move the ball off the pitch and in the air, made him very effective.

In 1936, he took 12 for 59 against Essex at Colchester and hit 69 against Somerset in just 26 minutes, including two sixes and 10 fours. In the match against Yorkshire, he hit 56 of the last 57 runs scored, When Middlesex totalled 127 – Smith coming to the wicket with the score at 32 for 8.

It is quite remarkable that a fast bowler who played for his country on five occasions, should be best remembered for his hitting. No matter whether he hit a fifty or scored a duck, his time at the crease caused great excitement. The only player to score a fifty in quicker time than Jim Smith was Leicestershire's Clive Inman who was being fed full tosses to bring about a declaration.

Smith made some remarkable hits at Lord's; a hit over Father Time against Lancashire; a shot through the Committee-room window in his first season; a one-handed smite off Yorkshire's George Macaulay on to the pavilion roof, over the Tavern and across St John's Wood Road and into a synagogue!

When Middlesex visited Hove, he arrived at the crease to find Alan Melville asking the ageing but still able Maurice Tate, 'Do you want a man out for Jim?' 'What-Skipper?' asked Maurice. 'With the new ball?' Melville smiled, 'Please yourself,' – the ball met the middle of Smith's flashing bat and after hitting the corrugated iron roof of the stand, it shot into the road and was retrieved half, way to the beach. The ball was returned to Tate by a smiling Melville with a thick coat of rust, tar and sand!

His main stroke (possibly his only one!) was to advance his left foot in the direction of the ball and then swing his bat with all his might. It didn't matter to Jim – a fifty from his bat turned many a game, equally so, he often swung wildly when only a few runs were needed for victory and his partner was well-set. His fame went before him, the Tavern used to empty in a magical fashion when the word went round that he was going in to bat.

'Big Jim' was alleged to have been greatly distressed on one occasion when he was given out stumped, as he contended that he had never moved his back foot in his life!

In 1938, 'Big Jim' Smith hit 69 in 20 minutes against Sussex at Lord's and then days later hit 66 in 18 minutes against Gloucestershire at Bristol – the first 50 coming in 11 minutes. This was the fastest fifty until Inman's smiting of full tosses. He took 107 wickets – it was the last time he passed the one hundred wicket mark, as he'd put on weight and his speed and venom had disappeared, though his accuracy was still there.

His one and only first-class century came against Kent at Canterbury in 1939. It was a fairly slow knock, coming in 81 minutes! He and Ian Peebles added 116 for the last wicket, Smith's share being 98. The score was 212 for 9 and he was on 3 when Peebles joined him. Rain interrupted play twice during his innings; three of his seven sixes soaring right over the tents which ring the ground at Canterbury opposite the pavilion.

Also in this his last season with Middlesex, he took 7 for 55 against Lancashire, including the hat-trick —his victims being Nutter, Phillipson and Lister.

Middlesex wanted Smith to go back after the war, but knowing that he couldn't do the same job, he played for East Lancs from 1945 to 1948 and after a few games with Blackburn Northern in the Ribblesdale League, he retired and took a pub, the Millstone in Mellor (occasionally frequented by the auhor!)

He died on 8 February 1979 at his home in Mellor near Blackburn aged 72, after being ill for some time.

MIKE SMITH

Born: 4 January 1942, Enfield
Played: 1959–1980

FIRST-CLASS MIDDLESEX RECORDS

Matches	*Innings*	*NO*	*Runs*	*HS*	*Ave*	*100s*
399	644	77	18575	181	31.64	37

Runs	*Wkts*	*Ave*	*Best*	*5wI*	*Ct*
1866	57	32.73	4-13	0	210

TEST MATCHES: 0

A slow left-arm bowler from Enfield Grammar School, Mike Smith made his county debut in 1959, taking 14 wickets and showing great promise with the bat.

Also during that 1959 season, he captained the Middlesex Young Amateurs. He had created a very favourable impression with his accurate slow left-arm bowling earlier in the season for Middlesex against the Indian tourists. In addition to his bowling, he had shown himself to be a redoubtable schoolboy batsman and he clearly had the makings of an above-average fist-class cricketer.

However, as with many teenage spinners, his early promise with the ball failed to materialise and he developed into a fine batsman, a brilliant fielder with a safe pair of hands and a very occasional bowler. What was strange in Mike Smith's case, was the length of time it took him to establish himself as a permanent member of the Middlesex side.

He had plenty of natural ability and yet it was 1967, some eight years after he'd made his debut, before he was awarded his county cap. Middlesex at this time, possessed an unusually large number of competent batsmen and with the exception of Russell and Parfitt, it was often said that it didn't matter in which order their first eight came to the crease!

In 1962, he scored 650 runs and averaged 27, but it was to be a few more years before he established a secure place in the side, when he and Russell opened the innings.

It wasn't until Pasty Harris left Middlesex to join Nottinghamshire that Mike Smith gained a regular place and came into his own. With the confidence gained from having a regular place and the considerable advantage of opening the innings, Mike Smith proceeded to produce runs in the quantities one expected from him. In 1969, the first year of the John Player League he hit 517 runs, with a top score of 103 against Surrey at Lord's. In 1970, he and Eric Russell had unbeaten stands of 131 and 140 in the game against Oxford University. He hit another century, 110 against Lancashire also in the John Player League in 1971. He was now batting with great ease and after topping the 1000 run mark in 1972, scored over 1500 runs the following season at an average of nearly 50. He hit two centuries that season, almost making it three, being dismissed for 99 in the last county match at Lord's against Yorkshire.

Despite the considerable number of runs and the centuries he had made, he was never chosen for a Test match or an official overseas tour. He was certainly on the verge of being included in a one-day international and the England squad, and must have come very close to making the 1974–75 tour to Australia. One of the reasons the top honour passed him by, may have been because of his unorthodox technique. His initial movement was so pronounced that he was often on the move across the wicket when he played the ball.

He was very proficient at forcing seam bowling off the stumps to leg and in Middlesex's first Benson and Hedges Final in 1975, he hit 83, although Leicestershire were easy winners.

He occasionally captained the side in Brearley's absence, whilst the Middlesex leader was on Test duty. Smith led with great imagination and one particularly remembers his performance against Gloucestershire in 1976.

Against spinners, he had the advantage of a long reach and was always willing to use his feet. He became an excellent judge of the quick single, which helped him and his partner to keep the score ticking over. This was evident in the one-day game; in 1976 he scored 105 against the Minor Counties (East) at Lord's in the Benson and Hedges Cup as he and Graham Barlow added 204 for the second wicket. The following season, he went five runs better, in establishing the Middlesex second wicket record in the Benson and Hedges Cup, when he and Barlow added 209 against Northamptonshire. Also in 1977, he and Clive Radley added 223 against Hampshire at Lord's for the second wicket to establish a new Middlesex record for the Gillette Cup in the quarter-final match.

After a disappointing season in 1978, he reasserted himself the following summer with over 1000 runs. He played just four matches in 1980, when, sadly, it was realised that his first-class career was coming to a close.

A most unobtrusive and dependable opening batsman, Mike Smith scored 18,575 runs in his career with Middlesex.

GREVILLE STEVENS

Born: 7 January 1901, Hampstead
Died: 19 September 1970
Played: 1919–1932

FIRST-CLASS MIDDLESEX RECORDS

Matches	*Innings*	*NO*	*Runs*	*HS*	*Ave*	*100s*
127	*195*	*15*	*5434*	*170**	*30.19*	*7*

Runs	*Wkts*	*Ave*	*Best*	*5wI*	*Ct*
10556	385	27.42	8-38	15	107

TEST MATCHES: 10

Greville Stevens was one of the greatest English schoolboy cricketers of all time. He came to the fore when he played in the 1st XI at the University College School from 1917–19. He was a fine batsman and a bowler of leg breaks and googlies. He played for the Gentlemen whilst still at University College School, batting at number 10, he scored 24 and 11 and took one wicket. In his last year at the University College School in 1919 he attracted special attention due to an innings of 466 in a house match.

He made his Middlesex debut in that 1919 season against Hampshire at Lord's taking 7 for 104 in their first innings and finishing with match figures of 10 for 136. He played in nine matches for Middlesex that season, scoring 198 runs, his top score being 62 against Surrey. He also took 24 wickets at 25.54 runs each.

In 1920, he gained his Blue as a freshman at Oxford, remaining a member of the side for the next three years, captaining the side in 1922.

In the 1920 game against Surrey at Lord's, Stevens came to the wicket with the Middlesex score on 149 for 6. He scored 53 helping Warner to take the end of the play score on the first day to 253 for 8. In Middlesex's second innings, Stevens and Warner added 25 in under 8 minutes as they took some very short singles; Steven's share being 21. This enabled Warner to declare on 316 for 7, setting Surrey 244 in three hours. Stevens came into his own, as he took 5 for 61 from 13.4 overs as Middlesex won the game by 55 runs. He ended the 1920 season with 44 Championship wickets at a cost of under 19 runs each. He took 13 wickets for 60 against Sussex that season, as Middlesex won by an innings. In all matches in that summer of 1920 Stevens scored 1357 runs and took 93 wickets, having a highly successful season for Oxford.

In 1923, Oxford beat Cambridge by an innings and 227 runs. Stevens took 6 for 20 as the Light Blues were dismissed for 59 in their first innings. He shone as a batsman too that summer, scoring 182 for Oxford against the West Indies and 122 for the Gentlemen at Lord's.

Against Yorkshire in 1925, Stevens hit 114 as he and Mann added 151 in

95 minutes – he was now knocking on the door of the England Test team.

The following season he scored 149 against the Australians, an innings that put him straight into the England side. He batted for five hours and 20 minutes and was ninth man out after opening the batting.

As the 1920 Surrey match showed, he was a good man to have in a crisis. He played 10 times for England, including the famous victory over Australia at the Oval in 1926. In the 1929–30 tour of the West Indies, his match analysis of 10 for 195 remains the record by any overseas bowler in a Bridgetown Test; his performance in the West Indies first innings of 5 for 90 was his best at Test level. His highest score at Test level was 69 against South Africa at Durban on the 1927–28 tour. Against the 1930 Australians Stevens dropped Don Bradman in the gully, twice in one Gubby Allen over. At the end of the over, Stevens told Allen to 'bowl at the bloody wicket'. When he was brought on a few moments later, Stevens almost immediately bowled the Don, turning to Allen he said 'I told you so'.

Greville Stevens was a classic-style batsman, making the most of his height in both front and back-foot play. In 1931, he and E T Killick added 277 for the first wicket against Warwickshire at Lord's.

He was an amateur who couldn't devote a great deal of his time to the game, yet he ranks high among the Middlesex players of the years between the wars. With a little more leisure, he surely must have become England's Captain and justified all the prophecies that were being made when he first appeared on the cricket field at the age of eighteen.

Dying on September 1970 at the age of 69, I suppose his ultimate record is of a promise that was never entirely fulfilled.

ANDREW STODDART

Born: 11 March 1863, Durham
Died: 4 April 1915
Played: 1885–1900

FIRST-CLASS MIDDLESEX RECORDS

Matches	*Innings*	*NO*	*Runs*	*HS*	*Ave*	*100s*
170	300	9	9255	221	31.80	16

Runs	*Wkts*	*Ave*	*Best*	*5wI*	*Ct*
4038	141	28.64	5-78	2	156

TEST MATCHES: 16

Andrew Ernest Stoddart didn't take seriously to cricket until he was 22 years of age, when he became associated with the Hampstead Club. He showed great form in 1885, hitting four centuries in the space of three weeks:

July 18	113	v	Hendon
July 2	108	v	MCC and Ground
August 4	108	v	Blackheath
August 8	120	v	Old Carthusians

So much so, that before the end of that season, he was playing for Middlesex, qualifying for the county by residence. He made his debut against Yorkshire scoring 3 and 21 though in the next match against Nottinghamshire at Trent Bridge, he hit 79 and 15.

On 4 August the following summer, he amassed the highest score then recorded in any class of cricket; 485 in 370 minutes, made out of Hampstead's 813 for 9 in a single day, against the Stoics (Later overtaken by the prodigious Clifton schoolboy Collins who hit 628 not out). His best strokes were his drives and his hitting on the leg-side. His total included an eight (four from an overthrow) three fives and 63 fours. What a day it was for 'Stoddy' – after playing poker all the previous night, he had freshened up with a swim, before eating a hearty breakfast. After his mammoth innings, he played tennis, went to the theatre and then finished the day with a late-night supper party!

He followed this innings with 207 against Blackheath three days later and 98 for Middlesex v Gloucestershire at Gloucester two days after that, giving him 790 runs in five days. He later hit his first century for Middlesex, 116 against Kent at Gravesend.

Andrew Stoddart was a typical Victorian amateur sportsman, though well above average in performance. He was a first-class hockey player, had a great flair for golf, could ride and box well, and was a great success at billiards. He was also one of the few men to have played for his country at both cricket and rugby. Between 1886 and 1893, he took part in 10 International Rugby matches and was one of only two men (A N Hornby was the other) to have captained England at both.

For Hampstead, he achieved some remarkable figures; between 1885 and 1907, he scored 13,912 runs (at 70.61). He averaged over a hundred in three seasons:

1887	(155.16)
1893	(111.00)
1899	(104.84)

In 1887, he played in the Centenary Match at Lord's and scored 151 for England against the MCC as he and Arthur Shrewsbury put 266 on for the first wicket. Versatility was the mark of men like Andrew Stoddart, who stayed in Australia after Lord Hawke's team had ended the cricket tour of 1887-88 to join the arriving English rugby side.

It has been said that Stoddart never played better than in 1890 for the South against the North. Facing Attewell, Barnes, Briggs and Peel, Stoddart hit 115 out of 169 scored while he was at the wicket. He was without doubt, a stylish right-handed opening batsman and a useful right-arm medium-pace change bowler. As a batsman, he would often attack the fastest of bowling, being a good driver and leg-side hitter.

Among his most famous innings was an unbeaten 215 made against Lancashire at Old Trafford, but critics at the time ranked his 87 at Lord's even better, for it was played on a fiery wicket.

He visited Australia on four occasions; in 1887-88 with G F Vernon's side; 1891-92 in a side led by Lord Sheffield (hitting a forceful 134 at Adelaide) and then in 1894-95 and 1897-98 when he both organised and captained the tours.

In 1893, he became the first Middlesex batsman to score a century in each innings. Nottinghamshire were the opponents in a match played at Lord's, Stoddart hitting 195 not out from a Middlesex total of 327 and then 124 in the second innings as the county won by 57 runs with time running out. He also hit a sparkling 125 against rivals Surrey – one of his outstanding achievements that season. He was the only man in the country that season to score more than two thousand runs, finishing with 2072 at an average of 42.28.

He captained England in W G Grace's absence and was the first captain in Test History to declare an innings closed. At the end of the season, Middlesex presented him with a silver bowl in appreciation of his splendid cricket for the county.

At Sydney in 1894-95, he became the first England captain to invite the opposition to bat in a Test. At Melbourne, he played a crucial innings of 173 and ended the victorious series with an average of 39.00

In 1895 playing for Middlesex against Surrey at the Oval, he scored 75 and 67. In his first innings, he was given out stumped, but the bail was not dislodged (so his innings of course continued) and in his second innings, a ball hit his wicket hard without removing a bail.

In 1897-98, he took another side to Australia, but before the Tests began, he received a cable informing him that his widowed mother had died. The unmarried Stoddart was so distressed he missed the first two Tests and then batted himself at No 8 in the next two Tests, before withdrawing from the final one. He played in 16 Tests, scoring 996 runs at an average of 35.57.

He had a good summer with Middlesex in 1898, topping the 1000 runs mark and ending with an average of 52.89. Probably his best innings that season was a fighting 138 with which he saved the match against Nottinghamshire at Lord's. It was thought that he might succeed Webbe as captain, but he played in only one game in 1899, scoring a duck, and the captaincy passed to MacGregor.

He reappeared in 1900, scoring just a single in the match against Sussex and then in Jack Hearne's benefit game against Somerset. After scoring 12 in the first innings, he batted for almost five hours in the second, scoring 221, the highest score of his first-class career – a wonderful end to his Middlesex playing days. He was one of the most punishing batsmen of the Golden Age.

His stockbroking business didn't flourish, though in 1906, he married a widow he'd met in Australia and took the 300-a-year sinecure as secretary of the Queen's Club. The following year, 1907, he played his last game for Hampstead, scoring a century against Old Westminsters. He had put on weight and was an ageing sportsman.

On 4 April 1915 at the age of 52, he ended his life in the manner of the disillusioned of his era, by putting a pistol to his head.

FRANK TARRANT

Born: 11 December 1880, Fitzroy, Australia
Died: 29 January 1951
Played: 1904–1914

FIRST-CLASS MIDDLESEX RECORDS

Matches	*Innings*	*NO*	*Runs*	*HS*	*Ave*	*100s*
206	344	24	12169	250*	38.03	26

Runs	*Wkts*	*Ave*	*Best*	*5wI*	*Ct*
17518	1005	17.43	9-41	89	193

TEST MATCHES: 0

Francis Alfred Tarrant was once a ground bowler at Melbourne, earning 30 shillings a week. He had first played for Victoria in 1898-99 when he was 18 years old. When Plum Warner was in Australia in 1902-03, he heard that Frank Tarrant was keen to make a name for himself in England and so it was he who began the negotiations that brought Tarrant to these shores to serve a two-year residential period for Middlesex.

Related to George Tarrant, the noted Cambridgeshire bowler of the 1860s, he began to build up a reputation for himself as an outstanding all-round cricketer during his two-year qualification period.

In August 1903, he first appeared for the Middlesex 2nd XI, making 47 not out against Essex before rain curtailed play.

He made his first-class debut for Middlesex in June 1904 against the touring South Africans, scoring 31 and 11. In his first county game that season, he made an impression against Somerset at Lord's, scoring 53 and taking 4 for 27 and 6 for 20, but apart from a big inning against Gloucestershire, he was unimpressive for the remainder of the season.

In fact, when Tarrant first played for the county there was much adverse criticism as to the importation of cricketers by Middlesex, but when his delightful talents shone through, this was soon forgotten. Tarrant was the most enthusiastic of cricketers; he enjoyed the game immensely, whether he was batting, bowling or fielding. He was at times, a rather cautious batsman, whose favourite shot was the cut. He was a left-handed bowler, bowling anything from slow to medium in pace. On a damaged wicket, and there were a few of those in Tarrant's day, there was no-one more likely to run through a side,

In his first full season, 1905, he scored over 800 runs and captured 60 wickets.

He was a player that would have graced any Test XI, but never did so, owing to the rules governing international cricket at the time.

In 1906, his figures were 1169 runs and 91 wickets, with his best bowling performances being 9 for 54 v Lancashire at Old Trafford and 9 for 57 against Yorkshire at Headingley. It was also the season when he took six catches in an innings against Essex at Leyton (a Middlesex record) completing 7 in the match.

By 1907 he was rated the best all-round cricketer in England and for eight consecutive seasons up until the outbreak of World War One, he accomplished the 'double' of 1000 runs and 100 wickets.

In 1907, his figures were 1552 runs and 183 wickets, becoming the first Middlesex player to achieve the 'double' for the county alone. He took 9 for 41 in Gloucestershire's second innings, including 4 wickets in four balls. He took 9 for 59 against Nottinghamshire at Lord's and 8 for 49 against Sussex to snatch a remarkable victory from the south coast county; Sussex only needed 96 to win, but could only muster 84.

In 1907-08, he visited Australia to play for Victoria. He played against the English team led by A O Jones and scored 81 and 65. He also played against England for a Victorian XI and hit a masterful 159. He was also in good form in the Inter-State games; his top score being 206 against New South Wales. His actions brought about a change in the laws governing registration. An amendment was made to the existing law on qualification, read 'A cricketer may not play for more than one county within the calendar year; the penalty for the infringement of this rule to be disqualification for two years. A British Colony or State, shall, for the purpose of this rule, be regarded as a county.'

In 1908, a touring Philadelphian side played Middlesex in a game that was completed in a day! The tourists were dismissed for 58 in an hour, thanks to Tarrant and The Hon C N Bruce and then Middlesex were bowled out for 92. In their second innings, Philadelphia were shot out for 55, with Tarrant ending the match with figures of 10 for 46 – Middlesex easily knocked off the 22 required runs (Patsy Hendren in only his fourth game scored 0 and 0). Tarrant started the season in brilliant form, hitting 157 in the first match, as Middlesex totalled 502 for 9 against Hampshire. He hit 144 against Nottinghamshire, Middlesex scoring 534 for 8 declared. Against Gloucestershire at Bristol, Middlesex won by 2 runs, Tarrant having a fine all-round match with an innings of 152 and 12 wickets for 149 (7 for 93 and 5 for 56).

The following season saw Tarrant perform the hat-trick twice, against Surrey at Lord's and Gloucestershire at Bristol.

As a batsman, he was primarily defensive, only developing his leg-side shots later in his career and only towards the end of his rather brief Middlesex career did he become the most aggressive driver in the side. H S Altham in his book *History of Cricket* rates Tarrant alongside Hirst as the finest all-round cricketer in the world, during the eight seasons leading up to the outbreak of war.

In 1910, Tarrant hit three centuries in his first five innings for the county, including carrying his bat for 140 not out from Middlesex's total of 262 against Sussex. The following season, he scored 2030 runs and captured 111 wickets; his best performance with the bat being 207 not out from his sides total of 378 against Yorkshire at Bradford, whilst with the ball he picked up another hat-trick against Somerset at Bath.

In 1912, Tarrant aided Middlesex to a four wicket win over Yorkshire by taking ten wickets in the match, including 6 for 73 in Yorkshire's second innings. His best match in 1913 was against Lancashire at Liverpool, even though the red-rose county won by an innings. He made 58 in Middlesex's first innings and then carried his bat for 81 in the second. Also that season, he took 15 wickets against Hampshire and 13 against Surrey.

By the 1914 season, he was at the height of his cricketing powers, scoring 1879 runs and taking 138 wickets. His highest score with the bat for Middlesex came in this his last season, when he hit an unbeaten 250 against Essex at Leyton – it was his fourth score of over 200 in England. The match saw Middlesex gain one of their biggest ever victories. Essex skipper Johnny Douglas sent Middlesex in to bat on a wet wicket – batting for 5 hours 20 minutes, Middlesex declared at 464 for 1. In his next innings after the Essex match, he scored 200 against Worcestershire and then triumphed in the match at Old Trafford against Lancashire, taking 9 for 105 and 7 for 71 and scoring 101 not out of the 145 runs needed for victory, which he and Harry Lee made without loss.

The War brought an end to Frank Tarrant's relationship with Middlesex. There is no knowing what his eventual record in the first-class game would have been. He coached and played in India, where he became the only other player (along with V E Walker and W G Grace) to score a hundred and take ten wickets in an innings. This he did, when playing for the Maharajah of Cooch Behar's XI at Poona, scoring 182 not out and taking 10 for 90.

He later settled in Australia, making a large income from buying and selling racehorses in both India and Australia, there being many Indian princes among his friends.

He played for Victoria in the winter of 1924-25 with considerable success and then after one unsuccessful appearance for the State the following season he retired from the first-class cricket scene although in 1935-36 under the auspices of the Maharajah of Patiala, he took an Australian team to India and played in one first class match.

The greatest all-round cricketer of the Edwardian period, he died in Melbourne on 29 January 1951.

FRED TITMUS

Born: 24 November 1932, Kentish Town
Played: 1949–1982

FIRST-CLASS MIDDLESEX RECORDS

Matches	*Innings*	*NO*	*Runs*	*HS*	*Ave*	*100s*
641	931	171	17320	120	22.78	5

Runs	*Wkts*	*Ave*	*Best*	*5wI*	*Ct*
50223	2361	21.27	9-52	146	378

TEST MATCHES: 53

Fred Titmus' promotion from the ground staff to the Middlesex XI had a story-book touch. It happened in June 1949, when Middlesex had Robertson, Compton, Edrich, Mann and Young all involved in the first Test against New Zealand at Lord's. They found themselves short so Robins and Allen visited the nets to look at the aspiring talent and collected Titmus. So instead of selling scorecards, he was in the Middlesex side at sixteen.

Just before his debut, he had played eleven innings for the Cross Arrows, scoring 660 runs at an average of 94.28.

When he made his debut against Somerset at Bath (where he scored 13 and 4 not out and bowled 2 overs for 9 runs and no wicket) There were repercussions, for the Secretary of the MCC had lodged a complaint regarding his playing. Later he was asked to accept the Club's apologies, which he did.

In his early days on the Lord's ground-staff, he was mainly an aggressive batsman, but before the end of his teens, he had become a dual-purpose bowler (opening with a few overs of medium-pace with the new ball, usually from the pavilion end – then switching ends to bowl off breaks; eventually concentrating on the latter). He could make the ball drift with spin and swerve so that it would often go away past off-stump for four byes. It wasn't until the late 1960s that he perfected his arm ball.

Titmus was fascinated by Jack Young and considered himself the right-hand version of him. In fact, there was a time when he had that little hop in his run-up that Jack did, though somewhere along the line, he lost it.

His career was interrupted by National Service in the Royal Air Force, but he played plenty of cricket for the RAF and the Combined Services.

In 1950, he took 45 wickets – a good performance in a Middlesex side that was struggling badly. He was awarded his county cap in 1953 and two years later became the first Middlesex cricketer since 1929, when Haig and Robins had achieved the 'double', to follow in their footsteps.

The summer of 1955 saw Titmus at the age of 22, establish himself among the leading all-rounders. His total number of wickets bounded to

191 at 16.31 and he nearly doubled his runs by scoring 1235 with a highest of 104. His tally of 158 wickets in all matches for Middlesex beat the previous county record set up by Albert Trott with 154 as far back as 1900 – a record which is likely to remain unbeatable! His best performance coming in the match against Somerset at Bath where he had match figures of 15 for 95.

Titmus was never a big spinner of the ball, relying more on craft and practising the arts of flight, pace and variation. He had a valuable ball that he ran away from the bat.

As a top-class off-break bowler, he turned in some good bowling performances. In 1956, he took 6 for 50 and 8 for 60 against Surrey, though Middlesex lost the game. In 1960, he took 8 for 89 against Worcestershire and the following season turned in figures of:

O	*M*	*R*	*W*
37.2	19	39	7

in the match against Surrey at Lord's.

Beginning in 1959, Fred did the 'double' in championship matches alone for four consecutive seasons, going on to do the double on eight occasions and taking 100 wickets sixteen times in all. In 1962, he produced the best bowling figures of his career, when he took 9 for 52 against Cambridge University at Fenner's.

As a batsman he was a more than capable middle-order player. There were countless innings for Middlesex when the back of the innings had been broken and Titmus arrived to stop the rot–getting his head down and fighting for the side and not for himself.

He was both determined and courageous and in 1964, opened for England with Geof Boycott who was making his Test debut.

In 1962-63 he was the all-round success of the England side in Australia. At Sydney he bowled 37 eight-ball overs, 14 maidens and took 7 for 79; included in the scalps were Simpson, Harvey, Booth and O'Neill. He ended the series with 21 wickets and a batting average of 36. Against New Zealand at Headingley in 1965, he took four wickets in six balls.

He had a deserved benefit in 1963 and though he was absent from the Middlesex side for all the Tests, he still took 72 wickets at 17.34 each. The following year, he missed ten county games, but ended the season with 101 wickets, partly due to a magnificent effort in the month of August. His best figures were 9 for 57 in the match against Lancashire at Lord's.

Titmus captained the county from 1965 to midway through the 1968 season, the period proved that he was a much better cricketer than captain. In 1966, he performed his first hat-trick against Somerset, when they were dismissed for 43 in their second innings.

In 1967-68 he was chosen as vice-captain of the England side to tour the Caribbean. After playing in the first two Tests, he suffered a boating accident, when his left foot was caught in the screw of a small boat and he lost four toes. Many believed his career to be over, but typical of the man, he showed great resilience and played at Derby in the opening match of the 1968 season in a specially fitted boot. He missed just one championship match and took exactly 100 wickets, including 6 for 5 in 13 overs against Oxford University and 5 for 11 in 18.4 overs in the match against

Worcestershire. He also scored 924 runs, narrowly missing another double.

In 1974 at the age of 42, he was sent to Australia with Mike Denness's side and was able to weather some of the hostile bowling by Lillee and Thomson, scoring a gutsy 61 on a fast Perth pitch. He represented England on 53 occasions, scoring 1,449 runs with a best of 84 not out made against India at Bombay in 1963-64. He took 153 wickets with that 7 for 79 at Sydney in 1962-63 his best.

After 1976, when he took 7 for 52 against Gloucestershire and 12 wickets in the match against Derbyshire, he retired to coach at the Oval. Having parted with Surrey for whom he played in one match, he returned to his Hertfordshire sub-post office, though he did return to play twice in 1979 and for a further five matches in 1980.

In August 1982, Freddie Titmus some three months short of his 50th birthday called into the Middlesex dressing-room for a cup of coffee. Mike Brearley having seen the wicket asked Titmus to play, which he willingly agreed to in borrowed kit. Middlesex beat Surrey by 58 runs, Fred taking 3 for 43 in their second innings. It was the only match in which he appeared – he had finally retired!

He had played for Middlesex in five decades before becoming Middlesex's Chairman of Selectors; he was also an England Test selector for three seasons from 1986 to 1988.

Fred Titmus is one of only five cricketers who have scored over 20,000 first-class runs and taken 2,500 wickets, only three players Wilfred Rhodes, Tich Freeman and Derek Shackleton have taken 100 wickets in a season more often.

ALBERT TROTT

Born: 6 February 1873, Abbotsford, Australia
Died: 30 July 1914
Played: 1898–1910

FIRST-CLASS MIDDLESEX RECORDS

Matches	*Innings*	*NO*	*Runs*	*HS*	*Ave*	*100s*
223	341	32	6253	164	20.24	6

Runs	*Wkts*	*Ave*	*Best*	*5wI*	*Ct*
20332	946	21.49	10-42	71	253

TEST MATCHES: 5 (Australia 3: England 2)

Albert Edwin Trott sprang to fame with some superb cricket against Stoddart's England XI in the winter of 1894-95, when he was only a few weeks short of his twenty-second birthday and already recognised as the most promising young cricketer in Australia. His debut at Adelaide was brilliant – he rattled up 38 and 72, both not out and took 8 for 43 in the second innings, England losing by 382 runs.

It was taken for granted that he would come to England in 1896, especially as his brother GHS was to captain the side. Inexplicably, he wasn't chosen (for which no real reason has ever been given). He never wore the green Australian cap again; but that was from his own choice. It is ironic that Trott's three and only appearances four his country produced these figures with the bat:

Matches	*Innings*	*NO*	*Runs*	*HS*	*Avge*
3	5	3	205	86*	102.50

He was understandably hurt, and aggrieved and so packed his bags and his massive 3 lb bats and sailed for England. When he arrived, after travelling with the official Australian side, he obtained a position on the MCC ground staff at Lord's and began a residential qualification period for Middlesex. While waiting to qualify, he played for the MCC occasionally and in 1897, took 48 wickets for an average of just over 14 runs apiece.

In 1898, his first season for Middlesex, he lost a whole month's cricket through an injury to his hand. In August, he took 74 wickets with 11 or 12 wickets a match being commonplace. On wickets that gave him the slightest assistance, he was virtually unplayable. Against Yorkshire, the eventual Champions, he took 7 for 13 in 14.1 overs, as the white-rose county were dismissed for 45. He ended the season with 102 wickets.

Without doubt, Trott's best two seasons were 1899 and 1900. In 1899, he scored 1175 runs and took 239 wickets and in 1900 he scored 1337 runs and captured 211 wickets in all first-class matches.

He had a superb all-round match against Sussex in May 1899, taking 12 for 200 and scoring 123 and 35 not out. His 123 included a massive on-drove off Fred Tate, the ball striking a projecting piece of masonry on the south-west corner of the pavilion. In July of that season when Trott faced his fellow Australians whilst playing for the MCC, he hit one ball from Monty Noble right over the pavilion roof, striking the chimney and bouncing away to end up in the garden of the dressing-room attendant – yet all he achieved was four runs!

His best century was the 164 he hit against Yorkshire at Lord's that summer, scoring his last 137 in an hour and a half. He hit 27 fours, many of which would have been sixes today. He put F S Jackson into the pavilion three times, two hits landed on the top balcony of the pavilion and one even found a way into the scorers' box.

In 1900, he bowled all eight batsmen in taking 8 for 43 against Gloucestershire at Clifton. It was in that 1900 season that he took in 14.2 overs (including 5 maidens) 10 Somerset wickets at Taunton for 42. He still had something special in store for Somerset .....

Although he took 176 wickets in 1901, he began surprisingly, to show signs of 'falling away', though only 28 at that time. He started to put on weight and became muscle-bound, no longer being able to bowl the extra-fast delivery that had been so deadly.

As a bowler, Trott was a genius at experimentation. It is reported that he practised his leg-break bowling at a wicket completely blanked-out by a large box placed on the batting crease. Only when Trott could turn the ball on to the stumps from either side was he fully satisfied. It seems he bowled everything from slow to fast. *Wisden* probably best summing up his genius with the words: 'Perhaps he may best be described as a pace bowler.' The meaning was very different from nowadays – he didn't bowl fast, slow, spin or swing! His famous 'surprise yorker' was his own personal secret-weapon; he was without doubt, the most inventive and original performer with the ball in first-class cricket.

Albert Trott was also a magnificent fieldsman, both in the slips and to his own bowling. It is reputed that Trott was something of a perfectionist. The story goes that a professional having lost a match through slipshod fielding, was seized by Trott in the dressing-room, put across his knee and soundly smacked with the back of a hair brush!

He was naturally, unable to play for England in Tests against Australia, but in the winter of 1898-99, he was a member of Lord Hawke's side that went to South Africa. Out of seventeen matches played, fifteen were won and two drawn. Trott's exceptional bowling was the mainstay of the team; he took 187 wickets at an average of 9.46 (they played against 18s' and 15s'). As well as appearing in Tests for both Australia and England, he played for Hawke's Bay in New Zealand in 1901-02 and achieved the match 'double' for them.

In 1907 in his benefit match against Somerset, he took 7 for 20 in the second innings; taking four wickets in four balls to dismiss Lewis, Poyntz, Woods and Robson, then a few minutes later finished off the innings with a hat-trick. Unfortunately, the game ended prematurely and it dawned on Trott that he had lost the best part of a day's gatemoney – a considerable amount of money!

In 1908 against the touring Philadelphians, he had match figures of 9 for 59, as Middlesex won inside a day.

He played his last match for Middlesex in 1910. For two seasons, he appeared as a first-class umpire, but ill-health caused his retirement early in 1913.

He was suffering from dropsy and had been in St. Mary's Hospital under the care of Sir John Broadbent when after a week, he couldn't stand it any longer and insisted on going home. In 1914, at the age of 41 he shot himself in the head and was found dead in bed by his landlady in his Willesden Green lodgings.

Albert Trott was undoubtedly cast to portray to perfection the role of the traditional tragicomic

ISAAC WALKER

Born: 8 January 1844, Southgate
Died: 6 July 1898
Played: 1862–1884

FIRST-CLASS MIDDLESEX RECORDS

Matches	*Innings*	*NO*	*Runs*	*HS*	*Ave*	*100s*
144	257	19	6064	145	25.48	4

Runs	*Wkts*	*Ave*	*Best*	*5wI*	*Ct*
3151	152	20.73	6-42	8	138

TEST MATCHES: 0

Isaac Donnithorne Walker was the youngest and for many the most talented of the brothers. He was at Harrow, captaining the XI in 1862 and 1863 and had even then played for Middlesex. In fact, he scored a century, 102 on his Middlesex debut against the Surrey Club at the Oval. He was hoping to go up to Cambridge, but the death of his mother whilst he was at Harrow prevented him from continuing his education.

As a batsman, I D Walker was a punishing player. He hit the ball hard, especially on the off-side. He possessed one unusual stroke – shaping up to play an orthodox drive, he would often send the ball over cover-points head to the boundary. It was nearly always safe, the ball travelling too much in the air for a fielder to catch.

In 1865, he hit a ball from Surrey's Stephenson clean out of the Oval, as Middlesex beat their rivals by 158 runs.

By 1868, he had jumped to the top of the tree; it was a year in which he had no superior as a batsman, save W G Grace. It was during this season that he played one of his best innings, scoring 165 for the Gentlemen against the players at the Oval.

He was sound in defence and a straight and powerful hitter of the ball. W G Grace described him as 'one of the finest amateur batsmen I have ever played with or against'. ID would only wear pads if a fast bowler such as Yorkshire's George Freeman was bearing down upon him in order to protect his shins.

The year of 1873 is generally regarded as the first year in which there was a county championship. Yorkshire were soundly beaten, with ID making 64 and 42 not out. He was the best batsman for Middlesex that season, scoring 392 runs at an average of 43.50.

As well as giving Middlesex notable service, he played and founded Harrow Wanderers. Although he was by nature an attacking batsman, he proved in 1874 against Nottinghamshire at Trent Bridge that he could defend, as he batted almost four hours for his 37 runs.

In 1883, he and Alfred Lyttleton put on 324 for Middlesex's second wicket in the match against Gloucestershire at Clifton, ID scoring 145. During that season, he scored 552 runs at an average of 34.

He had succeeded his brother Vyell Edward as Middlesex captain in 1873 and was excellent as a captain, although perhaps less tolerant than Vyell had been, he certainly fostered an enjoyment in the game. He had made up his mind that 1884 should be his last season, keeping to his word he handed over the captaincy at the end of the summer to A J Webbe.

I D Walker had been a powerful influence in Middlesex cricket. He took 10 for 72 in the first match against Gloucestershire at Lord's. He carried his bat through the innings against Surrey at Lord's, scoring 47 out of 126, he made 80 at Trent Bridge in the match against Nottinghamshire and averaged over 25 with the bat in this his last season. In his very last match, he hit 50 and 27 at Cheltenham against Gloucestershire; it was the last time a member of the Walker family took to the field for Middlesex.

It came as quite a shock to his colleagues that he had decided to leave the game, though ID reasoned that whilst he was still capable with the bat he was struggling in the field. The Middlesex players subscribed to a cup, which was presented to him to mark his retirement from the game and his great contribution to the Middlesex Club.

He died on 6 July 1898 at his brother RD's house in Regent's Park, the county match with Kent being postponed until August to allow the team to attend his funeral.

VYELL WALKER

Born: 20 April 1837, Southgate
Died: 3 January 1906
Played: 1857–1877

FIRST-CLASS MIDDLESEX RECORDS

Matches	*Innings*	*NO*	*Runs*	*HS*	*Ave*	*100s*
52	82	8	1310	87*	17.70	0

Runs	*Wkts*	*Ave*	*Best*	*5wI*	*Ct*
1813	120+10	15.11	10-104	13	84

TEST MATCHES: 25

Vyell Edward Walker was the fifth of seven brothers, born on 20 April 1837. He played his first match at Lord's for Harrow in 1853 against Winchester and made such an impression that he was chosen for the Gentlemen in their match against the Players at the age of 19.

In 1858, Middlesex played Kent, bowling out the hop county in their second innings for 47, Vyell Walker taking 6 for 31. It was reported in the local press that Vyell had a peculiar style of his own and that many of his victims were tempted forward so that they were stumped by brother John,

In fact, around that time, *Lillywhite's Guide to Cricketers* described Vyell Walker as the best all-round cricketer in the world. He was a fast-scoring batsman, but has often been cited as the best lob bowler the game has had.

In 1859, in the return match with Kent at Canterbury, Vyell Walker was again amongst the wickets, this time sharing them with Wells, probably George of Southgate. Also this year, playing for an All England XI against Surrey at the Oval, he scored 20 not out and 108 and took 14 wickets in the match, including all 10 in the first innings. He repeated this feat in 1864 when playing for the Gentlemen of Middlesex against the Gentlemen of Kent at Maidstone, the majority of his 10 wickets were clean bowled.

Vyell Walker shared the captaincy of Middlesex with his brother John in their first two seasons as a first-class county and then captained the side on his own until 1872.

He was an outstanding cricketer and in the first county game of that 1864 season at Islington, when Middlesex entertained Sussex, he produced a memorable performance. Vyell Walker took 9 for 63 in Sussex's first innings, though many (and that included his own team mates who congratulated him on the fall of the last wicket) thought he had taken all ten. Unfortunately, Charles Payne the Sussex batsman had been beaten by a delivery from Walker that had rebounded from Pooley the Middlesex wicket-keeper's pads and broken the wicket when he was out of his ground – the verdict, run out and not stumped. Undeterred by this, Walker proceeded to take 5 for 48 in the second innings to leave Middlesex the victors by an innings and 52 runs.

In 1865, when Middlesex met Lancashire for the first time at Manchester, Vyell Walker was again the hero, though the red-rose county won the match. In their second innings, Lancashire were bowled out for 178, Walker taking all 10 wickets for 104 runs from 44.2 overs. It was a record that stood until 1888 when George Burton took all ten wickets at the Oval in Middlesex's match with Surrey. Also in 1865 when Surrey entertained Middlesex at the Oval, Walker snapped up five catches in their first innings.

In the early days of Middlesex cricket, when the matches were played on the old Cattle Market ground at Islington, the Walker brothers practically ran the County Club. One of Vyell Walker's best years was 1866 when Middlesex won the Championship. In a couple of single innings' victories over Surrey he scored 79 at Islington and 74 not out at the Oval. He ended the season at the head of the Middlesex batting averages with 52.37 – this was an exceptional figure as the pitches were generally bumpy and variable and he like his brothers did not wear pads!

In 1867, a professional's pavilion was built; Vyell Walker had paid for it and he generously wished it to be considered the property of the Club.

In 1870, he broke one finger and dislocated another playing for the MCC against Nottinghamshire at Lord's two days before the first Middlesex match and was unable to play for the county during the summer.

He played his last game for Middlesex in 1877 at Trent Bridge as Middlesex came the closest they had to victory all summer. Nottinghamshire following on from Middlesex's 400, were 198 for 9 on the last day, still 10 runs short of making Middlesex bat again.

Vyell Walker was now 40 years of age and it was he who organised the England tour to Australia in 1878-79.

Ten years after playing his last game for Middlesex, he returned to the field for one special occasion, captaining the Veterans against the MCC during the MCC's Centenary Week at Lord's in 1887.

He continued to put a great deal of energy and enthusiasm into the game of cricket. He became President of the MCC in 1891 and was President of his beloved Middlesex from 1898 until his death at Southgate after a short illness on 3 January 1906 – he had occupied every important position within the Club.

The Walker's wealth had undoubtedly come from their brewery and when Vyell died, he left the princely sum of £1,598,177 – one cannot imagine too many cricketers leaving a sum like that!

PELHAM WARNER

Born: 2 October 1873, The Hall, Trinidad
Died: 30 January 1963
Played: 1894–1920

FIRST-CLASS MIDDLESEX RECORDS

Matches	*Innings*	*NO*	*Runs*	*HS*	*Ave*	*100s*
345	571	51	19507	197*	37.51	46

Runs	*Wkts*	*Ave*	*Best*	*5wI*	*Ct*
198	4	49.50	1-4	0	123

TEST MATCHES: 25

Pelham Francis Warner was born on the island of Trinidad in the West Indies on 2 October 1873, the youngest of C W Warner's eighteen children. His father was born two days before the Battle of Trafalgar and was for many years, Attorney General of Trinidad. Young Warner attended Harrison College, Barbados and by the age of 13 had gained a place in the 1st XI, but some six months later, he came to England.

He entered Whitelaw's House at Rugby, where he was in the 1st XI and captain in 1892. It was at Rugby that Pelham Warner developed into 'Plum' Warner and where he was coached by Tom Emmett, a notable Yorkshireman. 'Coom forrard Maister Warner.' Instructed Emmett, 'Coom forrard if tha's coomin' at all.' Plum wasn't a born batsman; he learned by trial and error and determination. He then went up to Oxford, where he was at Oriel College, but didn't get his Blue until his third year.

He hit 163 for the Middlesex 2nd XI and was invited to play in the matches against Somerset at Taunton and Gloucestershire at Clifton. It wasn't a sensational beginning, as he scored 6, 4, 14 not out and 29 not out.

In January 1897, he went on what was to be the first of many journeys across the seas, when he accepted an invitation by Lord Hawke. The opening match of that tour strangely enough was against Trinidad and Plum scored 119 – it was the first hundred scored on the island in an important match.

In the summer of 1897, he made his first century and the highest score of the season for Middlesex, 176 v Nottinghamshire, Plum ending the season with more runs than any other Middlesex player.

However, it was that trip with Lord Hawke's side that infected Warner with the travel bug. At the end of the 1897 season, he took a side to America and was only 23 years of age. He followed this in the spring of 1898 with a party to Portugal and then after the home season, took a team to America and Canada. In December of that year, he was a member of Lord Hawke's side to go to South Africa, where he scored an unbeaten 132 in his first Test at Johannesburg.

He had played for Oxford and so as an Old Blue of that University, he was qualified to wear the eye-catching cap of the Harlequins (dark blue, maroon and buff segments). This he did frequently, whatever team he was playing for.

By 1899, when he scored a superb 150 against Yorkshire he had established himself as one of the leading batsmen in the country.

In 1900, he hit 83 and 69 for the MCC against the champion county, Yorkshire and then 114 for Middlesex v Sussex and 146 against Lancashire – a superb start to the season. Unfortunately in this latter match, he sustained a rather nasty blow to the shin from a ball by Arthur Mold, it laying him up for three weeks. He played in 18 matches that season, scoring 1335 runs with five centuries and an average of 44.50.

In 1901, he hit his highest score for Middlesex, carrying his bat for 197 from Middlesex's total of 400 in the match against Somerset.

Inevitably, Warner captained the first MCC touring side which went to Australia in 1903-04 and won the Test series 3–2 against all the predictions. When he returned home, Warner was rewarded with a place on the MCC Committee.

He was a batsman of efficiency and neatness, a fine cutter of the ball good against spin and more than capable against the faster stuff. He showed a great tenacity when things weren't going for him.

In 1904 he scored 59 and 97 for the Gentlemen v Players at Lord's against a superb attack – Hirst, Lees, Rhodes, Arnold and Haigh.

In the wet summer of 1907, Warner was in superb form, scoring 1891 runs at an average of 46.12, finishing second in the national batting averages. Perhaps his best innings that summer was his 149 against Surrey at the Oval. By lunch, he had scored 115, as he and J Douglas went on to make 232 for the first wicket in two and a half hours!

He was the natural successor to Gregor MacGregor as Middlesex captain in 1908, holding the position until his retirement at the end of the 1920 season. He had another outstanding season in 1908, scoring 1298 runs at an average of 54.08. Representing the MCC against Yorkshire, he hit 64 not out from the MCC's total of 95 on a sticky wicket.

He was a good batsman and a great captain. He got the best out of his players by kindness backed up by firmness. He never stood for any nonsense. Once, a Middlesex bowler came to him before a match at Lord's, saying that he was afraid he wouldn't be able to play as he had damaged a finger in the nets. 'Plum' examined the finger, it was slightly bruised. 'Do you mean to say,' he asked the player concerned 'Do you mean to say that because of a mere bruise you feel you can't take the field?' Then he added 'A cricketer should be ready to bleed for Middlesex.'

Perhaps he can be best summed up as a shrewd captain, a brilliant tactician and an excellent judge of a player's capabilities.

In 1911, he scored 2123 runs at an average of 46.15; it was his best year. He reached the highest score of his career, 244 against the champion county, Warwickshire when playing for the Rest of England. He was chosen to lead England to Australia for the second time in the close season and hit 151 in the first tour match against South Australia. It was the only match he played in, as he was struck down by a serious illness.

He was popular abroad to the point of reverence and was admired by every team he ever led.

At no time Was he blessed by good health. 'Hey Maister Warner' said Yorkshire's George Hirst after he'd bowled Plum for fifty, 'If God'd only given thee a proper stomach tha'd a' been a Champion.'

He had recovered from his illness in Australia by the time the 1912 season was underway. He began the season by scoring three centuries within ten days, including a fine 126 for the Rest of England against the MCC Australian Touring XI. He played on a fairly regular basis in 1913, after missing the latter half of the previous season, ending with 987 runs at an average of 41.12.

During the First World War, he served with the Inns of Court and spent some time at the War Office with the rank of Captain, attached to the General Staff and then in 1916, entered hospital at King Edward VII for Officers for an operation.

He hit 101 in the match against the Australian Imperial Forces in May 1919 – it was the first post-war century, but he was attacked by cramp and was forced to retire, and had to be carried to the pavilion.

When the first-class game resumed in 1919, he was 45 years of age and considering retirement, but was persuaded by A J Webbe to carry on for one more season. As it turned out, it was to be a magnificent finale.

It was both dramatic and emotional as he led Middlesex to nine consecutive victories to capture the 1920 Championship, the last against Surrey at Lord's – it was a glorious victory, which 'pipped' Lancashire at the post.

During the whole of his first-class career, he scored 29,028 runs with 60 centuries and an average of 36.28. As *Wisden* said in 1921, 'There have been many greater cricketers than Pelham Warner, but none more devoted to the game. Whether winning or losing, he has always been the same.'

He had been called to the Bar in 1900, but he never practised law. From 1903 onwards, he made a profession of cricket journalism, beginning by writing a weekly column for the *Westminster Gazette*. In 1921, he began what was to be an eleven year spell as cricket correspondent of the

Morning Post. It was during this time that he became editor of *The Cricketer* at its inception in 1921, remaining in that post for almost forty years.

His retirement from first-class cricket did not mean the end of his touring. In 1926-27 he led an MCC team to South America and in 1932-33 went to Australia as joint-manager of the infamous bodyline tour.

In 1937, his outstanding services to cricket, both on and off the field were recognised by a knighthood.

During the Second World War, he was appointed Deputy Secretary of the MCC, soon arranging matches for the harassed public, who were able to see their favourites play again.

On 3 May 1950, he was nominated President of the MCC by the Duke of Edinburgh, though His Royal Highness in fact couldn't be present, and Lord Cornwallis presided in his absence. In 1953, the MCC gave a dinner in the Long Room to celebrate his 80th birthday. In 1958, a new grandstand built at Lords was named after him and three years later, he became the first life Vice-President of the MCC.

Known as 'The Grand Old Man' of English cricket, he died at West Lavington, near Midhurst, Sussex on 30 January 1963 at the age of 89. On Friday 8 March that year, his ashes were scattered at Lord's near the Warner Stand, close to the spot where he had hit his first four for Rugby v Marlborough in 1889.

Sir Pelham Warner was a man who played and watched more cricket than anyone has ever done or probably will do – a man passionately devoted to the game of cricket.

JOHN WARR

Born: 16 July 1927, Ealing
Played: 1949–1960

FIRST-CLASS MIDDLESEX RECORDS

Matches	*Innings*	*NO*	*Runs*	*HS*	*Ave*	*100s*
260	344	90	2744	51	10.80	0

Runs	*Wkts*	*Ave*	*Best*	*5wI*	*Ct*
14592	703	20.76	9-65	24	91

TEST MATCHES: 25

As a schoolboy, John Warr was evacuated from Ealing County Grammar School to spend the early part of the War years cycling each day from Wendover to Aylesbury. Later he showed great promise on the cricket field of which the Ealing Club was soon to avail itself. Despite all these interruptions, he won a state scholarship to Cambridge.

He then spent two successful years in the Navy, before refusing the offer of a commission to take up his scholarship at Emmanuel College, Cambridge. He began by taking many wickets at Cambridge, This came as a surprise for he had no previous reputation at school or services cricket.

In his first first-class match against Yorkshire, he took just one wicket, that of Ted Lester. Also making their first appearances that day were Brian Close and Fred Trueman. However, the bowling of J J Warr was to win matches and in the next match he took 6 for 35 against Lancashire.

By the end of the 1949 season, he had taken seven wickets in the Varsity match and 30 in the eight Championship games he played for Middlesex. They were an important factor in Middlesex tying for the Championship with Yorkshire. His best figures came in the last game that season, when he took 5 for 36 against Derbyshire.

He had raised the hope that for the first time since the war years the county looked to have a bowler of great promise. He was a tearaway medium-fast bowler – his action was poor, but he had great stamina.

During the 1950 season, he took 87 wickets, 21 in six matches on the perfect wickets at Fenner's and 40 in his vacation for Middlesex.

Surprisingly, he was selected for Freddie Brown's tour of Australia whilst still at Cambridge. He performed very effectively in the state matches, but was over-bowled in the two Tests he played due to injuries to Bailey and Wright. He thus ended his Test career as the most expensive wicket-taker in Test cricket (1 for 281) This was a record he retained until 1985, when Sri Lanka's Roger Wijesuriya's only wicket cost 294 runs!

He returned to Cambridge to complete his degree and captained the University in his final year. On his return from Australia, he had developed into a much more controlled opening bowler and his fielding too had improved.

As a bowler, he was a tireless right-arm bowler and would try to bowl as quick at the end of the day as he had at the beginning of play with the new ball. He had become part of a good opening attack with Alan Moss, taking 66 wickets in 1955 and then when Moss was injured the following season, 102 wickets in the Championship. In all matches that season, he took 116 wickets at 18.17, including 9 for 65 v Kent at Lord's and a hat-trick against Leicestershire at Loughborough. It was probably the first time when Warr did himself justice, bowling splendidly throughout the summer.

Playing for Middlesex throughout the fifties, he had developed a ball of considerable late out-swing, capable of beating the best batsmen. When at his prime in the mid-fifties, he was never considered for his country again, due to the likes of Statham, Trueman and Tyson.

In 1958, he succeeded to the Middlesex captaincy. In the last year of his leadership, the county finished in third position in the County Championship. John Warr was a most able captain – a shrewd assessor of men, both colleagues and opposition. He led by example, for having taken on a young side full of promise, he made them into an effective unit and an attractive side to watch.

He played his last game for Middlesex in 1960, a season in which he took 6 for 17 at New Road in the match against Worcestershire, He left first-class cricket at the end of the 1960 season at the age of 33, feeling that he must concentrate on a business career.

Over 12 seasons, he took 956 wickets at 22.79 runs each, 703 of them for Middlesex. The progress the county made under his guidance had been enormous.

During the winters whilst he had been playing, he'd worked in the discount market and on retiring as a player, he climbed the ladder in the City. He had many other interests, he was President of the MCC from 1987-88, a member of the Jockey Club and a senior steward at Goodwood.

As an after-dinner speaker, John Warr is sought after all over the globe. He possesses energy, enthusiasm and a great sense of fun, all of which shone through in his cricket.

JACK YOUNG

Born: 14 October 1912, Paddington
Played: 1933–1956

FIRST-CLASS MIDDLESEX RECORDS

Matches	*Innings*	*NO*	*Runs*	*HS*	*Ave*	*100s*
292	343	95	2124	62	8.56	0

Runs	*Wkts*	*Ave*	*Best*	*5wI*	*Ct*
22709	1182	19.21	8-31	70	125

TEST MATCHES: 8

Jack Young sprang from a theatrical background, his father being a celebrated comic. He was a slow left-arm bowler who was tried several times for Middlesex over a period of five or six years before the war.

The improvement he had made by the restart of cricket in 1946 was spectacular. He was so hard to hit, that less than 2 runs per over were hit off him.

In 1946, his bowling average was 16, when he turned in some marvellous performances against the Champion County Yorkshire – he took 4 for 41 and 8 for 31 at Lord's and then whilst representing the MCC at Scarborough, he took 8 for 33. This was also the season that he performed the first of his two hat-tricks against Northamptonshire.

He was on several occasions given the new ball and instructed to step up his pace for a few overs and make use of the seam, There is no doubt about it, these demands on his versatility certainly spoiled his figures.

He had a low flight and a quick break-away towards slips and certainly wasn't afraid of any punishment that the batsman might inflict. Coupled with this, he was a neat yet often spectacular fielder close to the wicket.

Jack Young carried a great weight on his shoulders, having occasionally to open the bowling. Yet he ended the season of 1947 with 159 wickets at 16.54 in all matches and 122 at 15.81 in the County Championship. He had match figures of 9 for 82 against Gloucestershire at the Cheltenham College Ground and another nine wickets in the match against Hampshire on a suspect wicket at Portsmouth. His best performance that season was 7 for 46 as Glamorgan were bowled out for 99 on a sticky wicket. He was selected to represent England in the fourth Test and though his bowling helped Middlesex to many a victory, he only played eight times for his country.

He was accused of being a 'defensive' bowler, for with his superb length, he rarely tossed the ball up to try to beat the batsman in the air.

He ended the 1948 season with forty wickets fewer than the previous summer and at a slightly higher cost, yet in his first three full seasons, he had taken 399 wickets at 17.50 runs each. He took 14 for 97 against Surrey at the Oval and against Kent at Lord's in a low-scoring encounter on a rain-affected wicket, Young took 7 wickets in each innings as Middlesex won by one wicket. At Trent Bridge, he bowled eleven consecutive maidens to Bradman and Hassett – no mean feat.

In 1949, he took 131 wickets at 18.49 each, his best performance being 7 for 47 against Kent at Canterbury, following it with 6 for 72 in the second innings. In the game against Lancashire, the red-rose county scored 304. Before a late-order batsman threw the bat, Young actually bowled 49 overs for only 47 runs – he finished the innings with 4 for 71. He also played the last of his eight Tests in 1949 against New Zealand at Lord's, turning in his best performance with the ball, 3 for 65. The following season, he was the only Middlesex bowler to top the one hundred wicket mark, taking 101 at 20.66. He was still bowling very tightly and in the 1950 season, he bowled 13 maidens in a row in Middlesex's match with Glamorgan.

In 1951, he bowled almost 300 overs more than anyone else in the country and was considered by most judges (except the Test selectors) to be the best of his sort in the land. His best performance was 7 for 44 and in the match against Lancashire at Lord's, he produced his second hat-trick. At Hastings that summer, whilst playing for an England XI against a Commonwealth XI, he took 9 for 55.

By 1952, Jack Young was suffering with knee problems and in June he broke a finger – yet he still ended the season with 137 wickets from 1298 overs in County Championship matches alone.

In 1953, he turned in another good performance against Kent at Canterbury, taking 14 for 115, including 8 for 60 in the second innings. The 1953 season ended with a tie at Peterborough, where Young took the last two wickets with successive deliveries. He headed the Middlesex bowling averages the following season and played his last game two summers later.

A short, genial man, Jack Young displayed slow left-arm bowling as a gentle art.

APPENDICES

Statistical Analysis

Whilst it is purely a matter of opinion as to how good a player a man is, or has been, and it is certainly true that figures seldom tell the true story of any cricketer, the author hopes the following will go some way to explaining why he has chosen the following eleven players as his team of *Famous Cricketers of Middlesex* though it was very difficult to leave out players of the calibre of Gatting, Stoddart and Trott.

1. Jack Robertson
2. J W Hearne
3. Bill Edrich
4. Denis Compton
5. Patsy Hendren
6. Pelham Warner (Captain)
7. Frank Tarrant
8. John Murray
9. Fred Titmus
10. Gubby Allen
11. J T Hearne

MIDDLESEX TOP TENS

The following section lists the best performances in each of several categories, showing in statistical form the 'Top Ten' for Middlesex.

Most Matches

1.	F J Titmus	641
2.	E H Hendren	581
3.	C T Radley	512
4.	J T Murray	508
5.	J W Hearne	465
6.	J T Hearne	453
7.	J D B Robertson	423
8.	N E Haig	417
9.	H W Lee	401
10.	W E Russell	400

Most Wickets

1.	F J Titmus	2361
2.	J T Hearne	2093
3.	J W Hearne	1483
4.	J M Sims	1257
5.	J A Young	1182
6.	F J Durston	1178
7.	A E Moss	1088
8.	F A Tarrant	1005
9.	J E Emburey	953
10.	A E Trott	946

Most Runs

1.	E H Hendren	40,302
2.	J W Hearne	27,612
3.	J D Robertson	27,088
4.	W J Edrich	25,738
5.	C T Radley	24,147
6.	W E Russell	23,108
7.	D C S Compton	21,781
8.	P H Parfitt	21,304
9.	P F Warner	19,507
10.	M W Gatting	19,291

Most Test Appearances

1.	D C S Compton	78
2.	M W Gatting	68
3.	J E Emburey	60
4.	F J Titmus	53
5.	P H Edmonds	51
6.	E H Hendren	51
7.	J M Brearley	39
8.	W J Edrich	39
9.	P H Parfitt	37
10.	P R Downton	30

Most Hundreds

1.	E H Hendren	119
2.	J W Hearne	71
3.	D C S Compton	67
4.	W J Edrich	62
5.	J D Robertson	59
6.	M W Gatting	52
7.	P H Parfitt	46
	P F Warner	46
9.	C T Radley	42
10.	W E Russell	37
	M J Smith	37

Most Catches (Fieldsmen)

1.	E H Hendren	562
2.	C T Radley	480
3.	P H Parfitt	452
4.	W J Edrich	382
5.	F J Titmus	378
6.	J T Hearne	306
7.	J D B Robertson	301
8.	J E Emburey	291
9.	W E Russell	274
10.	D C S Compton	264

Batting Averages

1.	M W Gatting	53.00
2.	D C S Compton	49.96
3.	E H Hendren	48.82
4.	W J Edrich	43.40
5.	J W Hearne	41.15
6.	W N Slack	40.53
7.	J D Robertson	38.37
8.	J M Brearley	38.33
9.	F A Tarrant	38.03
10.	P F Warner	37.51

Bowling Averages

1.	V E Walker	15.11
2.	G Burton	17.17
3.	F A Tarrant	17.43
4.	C I J Smith	17.75
5.	J T Hearne	18.24
6.	J A Young	19.21
7.	A E Moss	19.81
8.	I A R Peebles	19.87
9.	J T Rawlin	20.15
10.	G O Allen	20.64

There are other players with better bowling averages, but they haven't been included as they haven't either played enough matches or performed as a regular bowler to warrant inclusion as a *Famous Cricketers of Middlesex*

Highest Scores

1.	J D B Robertson	331*	v	Worcestershire	1949
2.	E H Hendren	301*	v	Worcestershire	1933
3.	J W Hearne	285*	v	Essex	1929
4.	W J Edrich	267*	v	Northamptonshire	1947
5.	M W Gatting	258	v	Somerset	1984
6.	D C S Compton	252*	v	Somerset	1948
7.	F A Tarrant	250*	v	Essex	1914
8.	W N Slack	248*	v	Worcestershire	1981
9.	H W Lee	243*	v	Nottinghamshire	1921
10.	S M Brown	232*	v	Somerset	1951

Also scored:

1.	E H Hendren	277*	v	Kent	1922
		240	v	Kent	1925
		234	v	Worcestershire	1925
		232	v	Nottinghamshire	1920
		232	v	Nottinghamshire	1931
2.	J W Hearne	245*	v	Gloucestershire	1927
		234	v	Somerset	1911
		232	v	Hampshire	1923
3.	W J Edrich	257	v	Leicestershire	1947
		248	v	Nottinghamshire	1938
		239	v	Oxford	1952
4.	D C S Compton	246	v	Rest of England	1947
		235	v	Surrey	1946

The following would normally figure in the 'Top Ten' but haven't been included, as they have not been classed as *Famous Middlesex Cricketers.*

D L Haynes	255*	v	Sussex	1990
C M Wells	244	v	Nottinghamshire	1899
A J Webbe	243*	v	Yorkshire	1887

BATTING AVERAGES (Up to the end of the 1990 season)

	M	Ins	NO	Runs	HS	Ave	lOOS
G O Allen	146	210	28	4667	155	25.64	4
G D Barlow	238	385	57	11640	177	35.48	23
D Bennett	392	590	120	10274	117*	21.85	4
B J T Bosanquet	123	200	13	6593	179	35.26	13
J M Brearley	291	485	68	15985	173*	38.33	29
S M Brown	313	549	39	15050	232*	29.51	20
G Burton	111	176	54	946	34	7.75	0
R O Butcher	237	373	35	10677	197	31.58	17
D C S Compton	296	458	49	21781	252*	49.96	67
N G Cowans	170	180	47	1227	66	9.23	0
W W Daniel	213	187	86	1043	53*	10.32	0
P R Downton	205	283	53	6670	126*	28.87	6
F J Durston	349	434	127	3569	92*	11.63	0
P H Edmonds	253	311	57	5037	142	19.83	2
W J Edrich	389	658	65	25738	267*	43.40	62
J E Emburey	292	372	73	7184	133	24.03	4
R A Gale	219	398	12	11234	200	29.10	13
M W Gatting	276	438	74	19291	258	53.00	52
N E Haig	417	630	39	12289	131	20.79	11
J T Hearne	453	630	223	4598	65	11.30	0
J W Hearne	465	744	73	27612	285*	41.15	71
E H Hendren	581	928	119	40302	301*	48.82	119
R W Hooker	300	442	71	8222	137	22.16	5
H W Lee	401	666	45	18594	243*	29.94	23
G MacGregor	184	286	39	4846	141	19.61	2
F G Mann	54	147	9	3403	116	24.66	3
F T Mann	314	472	39	10656	194	24.61	8
A E Moss	307	329	141	1234	40	6.56	0
J T Murray	508	761	105	15251	133*	23.25	11
T C O'Brien	156	268	19	7377	202	29.63	10
P H Parfitt	387	665	84	21304	200*	36.67	46
I A R Peebles	165	222	70	1361	58	8.95	0
J S E Price	242	191	80	902	41*	8.13	0
W F F Price	382	555	96	8300	111	18.08	3
C T Radley	512	813	132	24147	200	35.45	42
J T Rawlin	229	358	31	5680	100	17.37	1
J D B Robertson	423	745	39	27088	331*	38.37	59
R W V Robins	258	378	24	9337	140	26.38	6
W E Russell	400	712	54	23109	193	35.11	37
M W W Selvey	210	212	65	1835	67	12.48	0
J M Sims	381	515	96	7173	121	17.12	3
W N Slack	201	348	38	12565	248*	40.53	25
C I J Smith	152	216	23	2977	101	15.42	1
M J Smith	399	664	77	18575	181	31.64	37
G T S Stevens	127	195	15	5434	170*	30.19	7
A E Stoddart	170	300	9	9255	221	31.80	16
F A Tarrant	206	344	24	12169	250*	39.03	26
F J Titmus	641	931	171	17320	120	22.78	5
A E Trott	223	341	32	6253	164	20.24	6
I D Walker	144	257	19	6064	145	25.48	4
V E Walker	52	82	8	1310	87*	17.70	0
P F Warner	345	571	51	19507	197*	37.51	46
J J Warr	260	344	90	2744	51	10.80	0
J A Young	292	343	95	2124	62	8.56	0

BOWLING AVERAGES (Up to the end of 1990 season)

	Runs	Wkts	Ave	Best	5wI	Ct/St
G O Allen	8668	420	20.64	10-40	27	56
G D Barlow	66	3	22.00	1-6	0	130
D Bennett	19790	748	26.45	7-47	22	156
B T T Bosanquet	7271	268	27.13	8-53	19	91
J M Brearley	119	1	119.00	1-6	0	210/1
S M Brown	80	3	26.67	2-19	0	146
G Burton	9081	529	17.17	10-59	43	90
R O Butcher	159	4	39.75	2-37	0	256
D C S Compton	14124	477	29.61	6-63	16	264
N G Cowans	11480	503	22.82	6-31	19	38
W W Daniel	15089	685	22.02	9-61	22	52
P R Downton	9	1	9.00	1-4	0	436/58
F J Durston	25877	1178	21.97	8-27	65	230
P H Edmonds	20755	879	23.61	8-53	39	235
W J Edrich	9975	328	30.41	7-48	10	382/1
J E Emburey	23269	953	24.42	7-27	46	291
R A Gale	1525	46	33.15	4-57	0	108
M W Gatting	3349	125	26.79	5-34	2	261
N E Haig	24264	931	26.06	7-33	41	182
J T Hearne	38166	2093	18.24	9-32	171	306
J W Hearne	33309	1438	23.16	9-61	88	240
E H Hendren	2065	39	52.95	5-43	1	562
R W Hooker	13957	490	27.46	7-18	16	302
H W Lee	11064	340	32.54	8-39	7	164
G MacGregor	–	–	–	–	–	280/111
F G Mann	45	2	22.50	2-16	0	41
F T Mann	172	2	86.00	1-15	0	137
A E Moss	21566	1088	19.81	8-31	59	121
J T Murray	134	4	33.50	1-1	0	1024/199
T C O'Brien	272	2	136.00	1-10	0	111/2
P H Parfitt	6424	231	27.81	6-45	4	452
I A R Peebles	12122	610	19.87	8-24	40	120
J S E Price	16440	734	22.40	8-48	25	89
W F F Price	–	–	–	–	–	626/301
C T Radley	156	8	19.50	2-38	0	480
J T Rawlin	13277	659	20.15	8-29	34	159
J D B Robertson	2006	56	35.82	4-37	0	301
R W V Robins	14907	669	22.28	8-69	38	142
W E Russell	643	10	64.30	2-46	0	274
M W W Selvey	15653	615	25.45	7-20	33	56
J M Sims	31708	1257	25.23	9-92	77	202
W N Slack	632	19	33.26	3-17	0	139
C I J Smith	12001	676	17.75	8-102	39	69
M J Smith	1857	57	32.57	4-13	0	210
G T S Stevens	10556	385	27.42	8-38	15	107
A E Stoddart	4038	141	28.64	5-78	2	156
F A Tarrant	17518	1005	17.43	9-41	89	193
F J Titmus	50223	2361	21.27	9-52	146	378
A E Trott	20332	946	21.49	10-42	71	253
I D Walker	3151	152	20.73	6-42	8	138
V E Walker	1813	120[+10]	15.11	10-104	13	84
P F Warner	198	4	49.50	1-4	0	123
J J Warr	14592	703	20.76	9-65	24	91
J A Young	22709	1182	19.21	8-31	70	125

[+10] Number of wickets that bowler has taken where no analysis can be discovered,These wickets are not used in working out the average, but are included in the 5wI column.

WICKET KEEPING

	Matches	*Caught*	*Stumped*	*Total*	*Ave number of victims per match*
J T Murray	508	1024	199	1223	2.40
W F F Price	382	626	301	927	2.42
P R Downton	205	436	58	494	2.41
G MacGregor	184	280	111	391	2.12

The author wishes to thank Mr Derek Lodge for his help in compiling these statistics.